Mobile Cloud Robotics

by Patrick H. Stakem

(c) 2018

Number 4 in the Robot Series

Contents

Dedication

To James S. Albus, PhD, for his contributions to Robotics with his work at NIST and NASA, and for his insights on what the technology implied. He showed us how to get the work done, back when it was hard to do it. He dreamed of a better world, enabled by robotics.

Introduction

This book is about the topic of Mobile Cloud Robotics. Cloud Robotics emerged in 2010. This leverages the fusion of multiple technologies, such as the Internet of Things, mobile robotic platforms, Multicore Graphics Processing Units, and the Cloud platform. The Cloud concept involves virtual-izing the compute element, as we'll explain in detail later. Mostly, we will focus on mobile robots, as opposed to robotic assembly, and warehousing. At the heart of the problem is a computation-communication-power usage trade-off. We will look at the integration of these topics, with a roadmap and a defined architecture.

Cloud Robotics is an emerging field, enabled by the Internet of Things, the development and deployment of cloud services, and more capable small embedded processors with easier to use software, and better communication links. There has always been restrictions on the amount of processing, data storage, and communications we can put on a mobile platform. Early Mars rovers used more power computing their next move, than in actually doing them. The mobile platforms are usually power constrained, even if augmented by solar panels, and might have to return to base to recharge. Part of this problem can be solved by offloading computation to the cloud. Of course, this increases the power used for communications.

Cloud Robotics combines multiple technologies, including Cloud-based big data, cloud computing on demand, open source, data analytics and learning, and swarm behavior. Mobile Cloud Robotics assume the robots have a mobility platform. They could be service robots in a healthcare facility, or multiple-domain systems, land, sea, air, underwater, with the Cloud server in the field. Even robot swarms in Space are feasible, for both exploration of large and diverse targets in the asteroid belt, and for planetary surface exploration.

Closer to home, you may have sat in one, or ridden in one. Both Tesla and Google have self-driving cars that use cloud services. Tesla's Autopilot is in version 7.1 as of the writing. Google spun off their project to a new company, Waymo. Google's approach is to use remote cloud services to augment the onboard systems.

The Cloud-supplied services augment the more limited computation resources embedded in the mobile robot. It provides services on demand. These services can be related to data storage, downloading code, or computation. This allows a relatively simple and constrained architecture to have vastly greater resources. We will extend this concept. We can build a swarm of robotic platforms, not necessarily homogeneous, that can self-organize into a cluster computer, using, for example, the Open Source Beowulf software from NASA.

There is no reason the Cloud server has to be static, it can be a member of the swarm. The swarm members will share an architecture, differing only in their sensor payload (This is one usage model). The Swarm mothership can host the cloud, wherever the swarm happens to be. I use the termmothership here to indicate that the robot platforms are deployed from (and possibly retrieved by) the mothership. The mothership is a supernode, as members of the group or swarm are nodes. With the current generation of GPU-based supercomputer architectures, the mothership can certainly be a Cloud host. It shares the problems of power usage, and communication with members of the swarm. Depending on the operational environment, these issues can be addressed. The more real-time operations have to be handled locally, onboard the various members, due to communications delays. Up front, at the architecture level, the load balancing must be considered in a trade-off with communications and power usage. The mobile platform must always be able to meet the goals, even if a bit late. In some real-time scenarios, late means wrong.

Google's self-driving cars are cloud robots. The car has access to the database of maps and satellite data, The car send current data back to Google.

A Medical cloud, called a healthcare cluster, is beginning to be more popular.

"Cloud Robotics" first appeared in 2010. By 2019, there is a Google Cloud Robotics Platform.

Author

The author has a BSEE in Electrical Engineering from Carnegie-Mellon University, and Masters Degrees in Applied Physics and Computer Science from the Johns Hopkins University. During a career as a NASA support contractor from 1971 to 2013, he worked at all of the NASA Centers. He served as a mentor for the NASA/GSFC Summer Robotics Engineering Boot Camp at GSFC for 2 years. He taught Embedded Systems for the Whiting School of Engineering of the Johns Hopkins University, Engineering for Professionals Program, the graduate Computer Science department of Loyola University in Maryland, and Capitol Institute of Technology.

Mr. Stakem supported the Summer Engineering Bootcamp Projects at Goddard Space Flight Center for 2 years, and has done several summer Cubesat Programs at the undergraduate and graduate level.

Mr. Stakem can be found on Facebook and Linkedin.

Mobile Robot Domains

Mobile robots can operate in many domains. With some difficulty, they can be designed to operate in multiple, different domains. This section will discuss the unique challenges of the different environments.

Inside

The environment inside a building is more benign than outside, but can present its own unique set of problems. Bomb detection robots, for example, have to navigate (or be tele-operated) through a complex, structured environment. They may be called upon to ascend or descend stairs, a ladder, or even use an elevator. Generally, an inside environment designed for humans to operate in is rather benign. Warehouses can be structured to operate "lights-out." Inside a nuclear reactor, the game changes. It may have been a structured environment, before the reactor blew.

There have been three major incidents in nuclear power plants, in which teleoperated robotic devices were used to aid in reconnaissance. The United States, Russia, and Japan all found need of these alternatives to humans. Unfortunately, the electronics on the robots are as susceptible to radiation as human tissue. Most of these were tele-operated, with limited range. The sensor data of interest is radiation level, and imaging of damage.

Mobile robots can also operate in a health care or assisted living facility. Here, the robots are designed for that particular environment, and could easily be linked by mobile radio to a central cloud computer. Domestic assistance robots in the home environment could also be employed, using cloud services via wifi. Factories and large scale shipping centers have been using cloud robotics for some time now, quiet successfully. The following environments are "outside."

Ground/Underground

Ground based robot explorers can use a variety of locomotion. This includes wheels, treads, legs, etc. The Mars rovers tend to be 6 wheel vehicles, with each wheel operating independently under computer control. Legged locomotion is more complex to accomplish, but is more versatile in rough terrain. Hovercraft can be used, but they expend a lot of energy getting and staying airborne. They work well over ice, which is generally smooth, but not over sandy areas, where they create their own dust cloud. Wheeled systems are the simplest and easiest, although track is called for in difficult terrain. It is less energy efficient. Many wheeled, tracked, and legged platforms are available off-the-shelf in the marketplace. Larger systems might be derived from powered wheel chairs, carts, or vehicles. Larger platforms can also use re-purposed internal-combustion powered vehicles. The larger the chassis, the more the need for built-in safety.

One of the many projects of the Carnegie-Mellon University's Robot group was Dante, a robot designed to explore within an active volcano. Another project involved mine mapping. Both of these applications are autonomous, and communications for the mine mapping robot are limited, unless it drags a tether, which can get snagged.

Flight Platforms

Flight platforms come in several configurations. The lighter than air craft include balloon payload, and aerostats, or blimps. For heavier than air craft, the choices are fixed wing, and rotary wing. Big advances have been made in small rotary wing craft, leading to the 4-bladed hex copter, and 6-rotor devices. The rotors can be tilted individually for attitude control, or in combination, for vertical or horizontal flight. The advantage of winged craft is that they can glide. Kite-borne payloads can also be used, but they are mostly at the mercy of the winds. Flapping wing systems have also been demonstrated. There is, at the moment, a robot helicopter operating on Mars.

Flying explorers can cover a lot of ground, with an increase in the energy expended. Winged systems can glide, minimizing energy expenditure. Winged craft have found no off-planet applications so far. First, you need an atmosphere (rules out the moon), and enough atmosphere (makes Mars difficult). Balloon-borne payloads have been proposed for Jupiter, which, as far as we know, has no solid surface. For low altitude and short-to- moderate duration missions, the quad-copter or hex copter configuration is good. The energy expenditure is high, and they are not quiet.

A smaller and less expensive alternative is the Coyote drone, which has also been used in Hurricane research.

Lighter-than-air systems typically use helium for the lift. The are usually vertical systems, and they are at the mercy of the winds. Tethered balloon or aerostats can be also used. Very high altitude balloon platforms, free flying, can reach the fringes of space. There is sometimes a question of recovering the payload. Balloons are less expensive than heavier-than-air craft.

Aerobot is a term used for more sophisticated free-flyer packages. An Aerobot can be implemented in different technologies, heavier or lighter than air. Some lighter-than-air systems can stay aloft for 30 days or more.

Flying through Hurricanes is now routinely done by a dedicated cadre of pilots and crew, operating from southern Florida. The in-situ measurements they provide are invaluable to tracking and early warning of these storms. It is also incredibly dangerous. NOAA is now using unmanned instrumented drones in this role. They are expendable, have a longer working time on target, and provide more data. In addition, multiple units can give reading from different locations simultaneously.

Flying drones have been used to locate and identify sites of archaeological interest in Peru since 2013. Due to performance issues at altitudes above 12,000 feet in the Andes, drone blimps have more recently been used. The collected data is then used to compile 3-d maps that are then used to guide field surveys. These have found application in Mayan city sites in the dense jungle in Central America as well. Most of these bring back large volumes of data with them, to be processed when they return.

Water/underwater

Water-based systems can be limited to surface, or can be designed for sub-surface operations as well.

Smart buoys, floating data platforms, can be tethered or drifting. Vast networks of smart drifting buoys are returning data on currents, ocean temperature and salinity, and other data for that ¾ of the planet we don't have complete data for. They are generally solar powered.

For submersibles, the farther you go down, the more the pressure increases, and the greater the problem in keeping the water out of the vehicle. That having been said, submersibles have been to the deepest part of the ocean, and imaged weird life forms that thrive near volcanic vents. The further you want to go down, the more expensive it is going to be. Platforms tend to be very specialized. The oil industry is a major customer for the commercial units, ROV's, or remotely operated vehicles, with grippers and arms. These are telerobots, operated from the surface.

There is an interesting open source project called OpenROV that involves a do-it-yourself fairly low cost telerobot underwater explorer. I would like someone in Australia to put a couple of these at the Great Barrier Reef, and allow teleoperation via the Internet. Rent by the hour. They I could enjoy the reef environment without going all the way to Australia. Or, learning to swim. If one of you Aussies implement this, let me know, and give me one hour free, please.

RoboEarth is a European Union project framework for cloud robotics. It has a cloud robotics infrastructure, the RoboEarth Cloud Engine, which provides an infrastructure to link multiple robots and the Cloud server.

Under Ice

NASA sponsored the Robotics Institute at Carnegie Mellon University to build the Nomad Rover, a 4-wheeled, 1,600 pound autonomous explorer. It was deployed in Antarctica in the year 2000. It's job is to find meteorites. It turns out, a lot of the meteorites found in Antarctica are from Mars, based on their chemical composition. Nomad is doing the a similar job on Earth to what the Mars Rovers are doing on Mars.

Nomad is equipped with a laser rangefinder, high resolution cameras, onboard computer, satellite data link, and a gasoline-powered generator. It is looking for meteorites on the ice with a specific set of characteristics. If one is detected, it navigates to the target for a closer look. It has an arm with a camera and spectrometer, as well as a metal detector. If the rock meets the profile of being a potential meteorite, the GPS location is logged. The robot does not collect samples, but does sort through rock fields for items of interest.

A rock the size of a potato (Allan Hills 84001) found in Antarctica in 1984 definitely came from Mars, and had chemical and fossil evidence of life. It is yet to be proven whether this definitely shows the past presence of life on Mars.

Of interest is the ice-water interface, and under-ice exploration by a submersible, acting in concert with a ground vehicle.

Inside the Volcano

The Robotics group at Carnegie-Mellon University is headed by the famed Red Whittaker, who lead the CMU team to win the DARPA Challenge. He is also heading the team focused on the Google Lunar X Prize. One of his many projects was a mobile platform, Dante, designed to enter an active volcano.

In December of 1992, Dante and his support team ventured to active Mount Erebus in Antarctica, 12,450 feet high, and about 800 miles from the pole. Erebus is important enough that manned attempts were made to enter the caldera, all unsuccessful. How much the volcano contributes to the hole in the ozone layer above Antarctica is not known. The ozone layer blocks ultraviolet light from the sun, and is critical to the continuance of life on Earth. The robot made the descent to the crater floor, some 850 feet from the top. Here it took temperature measurements, and gas samples. Erebus tends to erupt in a minor fashion several times a day.

This was a NASA Project, supported by the National Science Foundation. The temperature proved to be around 1,100 degrees from the corrosive gases vented by the volcano.

Dante is a six-legged walking robot, weighing close to 1000 pounds, and connected to the support team outside the volcano by a tether to provide power and data, and possible retrieval if the robot becomes disabled.

In August of 1994, an upgraded version of the robot, Dante 2, explored an active Alaskan volcano, Mount Spurr. This is located some 80 miles west of Anchorage. The descent into the caldera was 650 feet. The robot was monitored from a control facility in Anchorage, via a satellite link, providing a live video feed.. Dante-2 was bulked up at 1,700 pounds, having been redesigned based on the earlier robot's lessons-learned. It was able to explore underneath a rock ledge, that had blocked an aerial view of a part of the crater. After successfully completing its mission, the robot walked its way out of the crater.

CMU Rovers have also been used in mine mapping. A rover called Groundhog went into an abandoned Pennsylvania coal mine and sent out live video to a conference on Mine Safety in 2002. They primary usage for the robots is seen as mapping. After initial tests, the concept of a wheeled rover was reconsidered, and an amphibious robot was designed. This is because old mines are frequently flooded.

Multi-Domain Systems

Multiple domains systems have enhanced flexibility, at the cost of complexity. We can have, for example, a ground based system that can launch and recover a drone or aerostat. This provides a "god's eye view" of the area around the ground vehicle. This is useful for navigation and obstacle avoidance. We can also have an amphibious vehicle, that is equally mobile on the land, and water. Another multi-domain exploration vehicle might be deployed on an ice field, and drill through the ice to deploy a submersible. That would be useful on the icy moons of Jupiter and Saturn.

Cooperative systems

Rover systems can operate cooperatively in different domains. We are talking here of non-homogeneous units, designed to different sets of requirements. We might have a ground vehicle that could deploy a smaller scout vehicle. That would be useful in underground exploration and search and rescue as well as indoors. The larger vehicle might not be able to climb stairs, for example. We might have a ground vehicle being able to launch an air vehicle, to fly ahead and define areas of interest, or of danger, for the ground vehicle. This is happening on Mars right now. There are many advantages to having an "eye in the sky." This introduces the problem of having the air unit find the ground unit for a safe return landing. This is easily solved with a beacon system or GPS navigation (where available). The ground system would recharge the air asset's batteries upon landing via an umbilical or induction. The air system would be short range, and would need to be capable of vertical take-off and landing; i.e., a quadcopter. The ground based systems might also deploy and retrieve a tethered balloon.

The concept is termed cooperative autonomy, and extends from cooperation between and among agents and systems, to human-machine interaction (as in the case of tele-operation). Virtual sensor platforms can be enabled, where different platforms cooperate on simultaneous observations of the target.

Similarly, a waterborne systems could also make use of an air asset or deploy a submersible. In one scenario, the waterborne systems goes to a predetermined location on a body of water such as a lake or bay, and deploys a small submarine craft for bottom sampling.

Drones or balloons can serve as communication relays for ground or water-based systems.

Space

In one sense, all satellites are robots. They are remote sensing platforms, or platforms that provide services such as Navigation and television. They have computers, and are fairly autonomous. One of the more popular standard platforms is the Cubesat.

A Cubesat is a small, affordable satellite that can be developed and launched by college, high schools, and even individuals. The specifications were developed by Academia in 1999. The basic structure is a 10 centimeter cube, (volume of 1 liter) weighing less than 1.33 kilograms. This allows multiples of these standardized packages to be launched as secondary payloads on other missions. A Cubesat dispenser has been developed, the Poly-PicoSat Orbital Deployer, P-POD, that holds multiple Cubesats and dispenses them on orbit.

Cubesats began as teaching tools, and remain in that role, although their vast numbers in orbit showed they they have become mainstream.

In what has been called the Revolution of Smallsats, Cubesats lead the way. They represent paradigm shifts in developing space missions, opening the field from National efforts and large Aerospace contractors, to individuals and schools.

Swarms

Swarms are groups of units, operating as a swarm as found in nature. Here, multiple units act with collective behavior, as if one mind. The behavior is seen in insects, birds, and fish. Use of a common hardware and software architecture for all swarm members is desirable. Only the sensor sets will be unique. The mothership provides cloud services to the swarm. The mothership can actually use the same standardized architecture as the swarm members, but may need enhanced power and communications capability. The compute architecture could be a cluster. It is even possible to allow a "cluster of convenience" to form, using the individual robot platforms to come together over a wireless communication network. The resultant collection is scalable to fit the problem at hand,

This section describes an approach where collections of smaller co-operating systems that can combine their efforts and work as ad-hoc teams on problems of interest.

A robot Swarm is based on the collective or parallel behavior of homogeneous systems. This covers collective behavior, modeled on biological systems. Examples in nature include migrating birds, schooling fish, and herding sheep. A collective behavior emerges from interactions between members of the swarm, and the environment. The resources of the swarm can be organized dynamically.

In Swarm systems, the key issues are communication between units, and cooperative behavior. The capability of individual units does not much matter; it is strength in numbers. Ants and other social insects such as termites, wasps, and bees, are models for swarm behavior. Self-organizing behavior emerges from decentralized systems that interact with members of the group, and the environment. Swarm intelligence is an emerging field, and swarm robotics is in its infancy.

Each member of the swarm will need to be aware of other members in close proximity. This can be facilitated by having the mothership be the center of the coordinate system. It will also maintain, as part of its onboard database, the location of all other members. It will also monitor for pending collisions and warn the participants. There will be rules concerning how close swarm members can get, a virtual zone of exclusion. All human interaction with the swarm wiould be through the mothership.

Each swarm member can monitor its own status, and this will be kept in an electronic data sheet format. This data will be kept locally, and updated to the mothership periodically or upon demand. The mothership will keep a database of the status of all units. The EDS contains two part, static and dynamic data. The static data is a description of the unit, a unique unit identifier, and its sensor and computer capability. The dynamic data contains operating parameters such as battery voltage and state of charge, unit temperature, a time stamp, and error codes.

The ground-based swarm will implement proximity-operations (prox-ops) in a more leisurely fashion, in that motion will be two-dimensional and at low speed.

Using standard clustering software, the swarm members will be able to form an ad-hoc "swarm of convenience" to process science data in-situ, to reduce downlink bandwidth.

A swarm of robots has a similar architecture to the vastly larger Internet of Things (IoT). There are platforms with embedded computers and communication capabilities, using the Internet for connectivity. The IoT platforms do sensing and control functions, and are now off-the-shelf, plug-and-play. The IOT devices implement an event-driven architecture. Right now, the IoT world lacks a good set of standards to ensure inter-operability. There are also issues of security for the IoT.

Swarm Space Missions

Let's talk about the birds and the bees for a moment. These groupings of animals exhibit what is termed swarm behavior, also seen in certain species of fish. This means the group moves as if one mind. So we have a group of homogeneous individuals, operating as one big virtual organism, a kind of spontaneous collective intelligence. It has its value in deterring predators, and hunting/feeding. A behavior emerges in the organisms' interactions, and their interaction with the environment.

An agent, in the computer sense, is an autonomous entity that senses its environment, and is goal-seeking. It can also learn. An agent may be implemented in software, or can be a separate hardware-software system.

We can use this cooperative behavior model in the control of a group of homogeneous robot systems. Swarm dynamics can be applied to coordinate multi-rover systems. First, the individual robots need to be aware of each other, and should be able to communicate. We don't need any one in charge. It is ad hoc groupings of diverse individual that come together to work on the same problem. Scalability extends to very large numbers of units.

This is a research topic, beginning to be implemented and deployed. A swarm of small spacecraft has been proposed for asteroid exploration. There are a lot of asteroids, thousands of them, between the orbits of Mars and Jupiter, perhaps the debris of a planet. Each seems to be very different. The trick is to find the gold one.

In the Swarm architecture, there is a mothership/dispenser. The mechanical design is straightforward. The dispenser has propulsion and electrical power section at the launch vehicle interface end. The avionics and data storage are located in the nose of the vehicle while deployers are along the sides.

The Mothership transports the units unpowered. Every day or week (tbd), the units are powered on, one at a time, and checked for functionality. The onboard database is updated as required.

After another system check of itself and the units, the Mothership deploys a series of generic scouts on a reconnaissance mission, to seek out areas of interest. The Mothership deploys units with broad spectral sensing. Based on their findings, the mothership will deploy additional units with specific instrumentation to the area of interest.

There are two main aspects which is involved in communication within a swarm network, the Network Topology and the Inter-Unit Link (IUL). These are explained below, and we expect to use standardized protocols.

Once a set of Units are deployed, the first challenge will be the initialization of the swarm communication network. This includes three main areas of implementation: Addressing, network discovery and synchronization. Gossip protocol can be the most appropriate, primarily because the underlying network is unstructured in its distribution of nodes. It is a robust way to bring controlled network initialization in a large cluster, in a decentralized manner. Each node will send out network initialization data to a fixed number of other nodes, where it propagates through the system, node by node like an epidemic virus in a biological community. Eventually, data is propagated to every node in the network, creating a global network map with very limited local interactions.

Additionally, every cluster will have a cluster head, which has the responsibility of streamlining the data distribution and associated tasks. Two or more Units in a cluster can be designed to back-up as a cluster head, in case the primary one fails.

The second important point of consideration in an IUL are the limiting constraints, which include size and power output. Satellites will exchange two types of data through its communication channel: primary observational data, along with secondary data which will include metadata, position, localization, and timing information.

Communication will be implemented on Ultra High Frequency (UHF). With the clustering and non-clustering topology, an inter-satellite communication range of 90km to 100km is viable for UHF within the power output range of 4-5 W. The next challenge is regarding selection of the ideal antenna and communication protocol, keeping in mind the existing power and mobility constraints along with the trade-off between radio power and communication distance. NASA's Nodes (Network & Operation Demonstration Satellite) mission, similar in structure to the Edison Demonstration of Smallsat Networks (EDSN) mission, deployed a satellite swarm of CubeSats from the ISS to test inter-satellite communication capabilities in 2015. A primary UHF radio was used for crosslink communication, and a further UHF beacon radio was used for transmitting real time health information of the satellite. In addition to this, position, navigation and tracking information can complement the primary data load. Optical communication may also be used.

We will now discuss several target missions in the Space Domain that would be ideally addressed by Swarms.

Asteroid Belt Mission

Use of a common hardware and software architecture for all swarm members, to the greatest extent possible, is essential. Only the sensor sets will be unique. A standard platform for the hardware, and standard software software will be base-lined. The mothership provides cloud services to the swarm, as well as transportation, checkout, database services and communications back to Earth.

Each member of the swarm needs to be aware of other members in close proximity. This will be facilitated by having the mothership be the center of the coordinate system. It can determine its position by celestial navigation. For the other cubesats, it can use a standard NASA ranging code.
(http://www.amsat.org/amsat/articles/g3ruh/123.html).

The mothership can determine its own location, on Earth, using GPS. In space, it can take star readings. It will also maintain, as part of its onboard database, the location of all other members. It will also monitor for pending collisions and warn the participants. There will be rules concerning how close swarm members can get, a virtual zone of exclusion. All human interaction with the swarm will be through the mothership. Due to communication delays, operation of the swarm by teleoperation from Earth is not feasible.

Using standard clustering software, the swarm members will be able to form an ad-hoc "swarm of convenience" to process science data in-situ. In addition, the mothership provides cloud services for communication, storage, and computation.

Mars Surface Mission

In the planetary surface scenario, the lander vehicle will serve as the mothership. It will have a more limited capacity to hold swarm members. All of these are rovers, with the lander serving as a communications relay, and a navigation point. An aerial member of the swarm may be included, to serve as a "gods-eye" view, and to target locations for direct exploration, maybe a comm relay. The air is thinner than on Earth, so drones are a problem, not unsolvable

The ground based swarm will implement proximity operation (prox-ops) in a more leisurely fashion, in that motion will be two-dimensional and at low speed.

The Mothership/Lander on the surface of Mars deploys rovers, that return to get recharged, and do data dumps. There will be an RF-based recall mechanism from lander/base to rovers, in case of a pending sandstorm. Rovers will transmit/receive on the go.

The Lander/base communicates with the rovers via UHF, not necessarily line-of-sight. The location of the horizon on Mars is closer, and we may need to deploy a tower antenna or maybe a balloon to pull the antenna up. Rovers communicate with each other via the lander/base. High speed data comm is not necessary, as rovers will dump their science data to the lander when they are back inside, via bluetooth or a hardwire cable connection. Lander position on the surface can be determined by sighting the sun, and the Martian moons. The current on-orbit imaging resources might not be able to detect the lander.

Standard Mars protocols are used from the lander to and existing Mars Orbit Comm relay, then NASA takes care of the transmission back to Earth.

Cooperative and hybrid systems

Rover systems can operate cooperatively in different domains. We are talking here of non-homogeneous units, designed to different set of requirements. We might have a ground vehicle that could deploy a smaller scout vehicle. That would be useful in underground exploration and search and rescue as well as in a warehouse. The larger vehicle might not be able to climb stairs, for example. We might have a ground vehicle being able to launch an air vehicle, to fly ahead and define areas of interest, or of danger, for the ground vehicle. There are many advantages to having an "eye in the sky." This introduces the problem of having the air unit find the ground unit for a safe return landing. This is easily solved with a beacon system or GPS navigation. The ground system could recharge the air asset's batteries upon landing via an umbilical or induction. The air system would be short range, and would need to be capable of vertical take-off and landing; i.e., a quad-copter. The ground based systems might also deploy and retrieve a tethered balloon.

The concept is termed cooperative autonomy, and extends from cooperation between and among agents and systems, to human-machine interaction (as in the case of tele-operation). Virtual sensor platforms can be enabled, where different platforms cooperate on simultaneous observations.

Similarly, a waterborne systems could also make use of an air asset. The water borne system could also deploy a submersible. In one scenario, the waterborne systems goes to a predetermined location on a body of water such as a lake or bay, and deploys a small submarine craft for bottom sampling.

Drones or balloons can serve as communication relays for ground or water-based systems. In planetary mission, particularly those related to the numerous moons of the gas giants, a hybrid mission would be required, where a lander deploys a submersible through the ice sheet.

Platforms

Many standard tracked, wheeled, and legged platforms are available for robots, as well as conventional model aircraft and rotating wing aircraft on the Quad-copter pattern. Many radio-controlled models, boats, submersibles, electric aircraft, cars, and trucks are readily available and inexpensive. These serve as the mobility platforms for integrating computational, sensor, and communication packages. These might be adequate for the job, or at least the proof-of-concept prototype.

Platforms can be all-wheel drive, or just several of the wheels can be driven, with idlers at the other positions for stability. One unique approach is to have a self-balancing platform with one large ball. Self-balancing mobility platforms, starting with the Segway, have made this technology off-the-shelf.

Actuators such as motors can themselves have built-in embedded computers. These are referred to as smart actuators. They may incorporate a local feedback and monitoring loop. IEEE-1451 is a set of standards for interfacing smart sensors and smart actuators. The standards cover functions, communication protocols, and formats.

Platforms provide the mobility in whatever domain we choose. The electronics for motor drive, battery maintenance, and communications can be common. The electronics is simple in most cases. The difficult part is path planning. This higher level function might be done on a cloud platform, or we can upgrade the Platform's compute architecture to a GPU. The mobility system, under the platform varies. The third part of the system is the sensor set. These can be unique for each platform, or they can vary. A computer may be included on the sensor platform to coordinate the sensors and handle the data. For example, a camera system may include the Raspberry Pi with its image processing pipeline.

Mobile Robotics

We will assume here we are talking about a mobile robot system, servicing as an autonomous sensor platform, in any domain of choice, possibly operating alone, or as a member of an organized group, or swarm.. What are the requirements for that device? First, it must have sufficient computational resources, not all of which need be on the platform, if it has cloud resources available. This includes computational resources, ans storage resources. Secondly, for the domain and the nature of the problem, we specify a sensor set. Then, it will require communication resources, particularly if it needs to connect to the Internet, for Cloud services. Ideally, the hardware and software architectures will be implemented with Open Source, off-the-shelf modules. This will ensure rapid develop and testing, to best practices. We also need to consider the requirement for self-testing, evaluation, and possibly repair. The device may have a requirement for manipulation, such as sample gathering. Last, but not least is the requirement for power.

Mobile Robot Computing Hardware

This section discusses the hardware elements of the Mobile Robot. Generally, we can think of the robot system as consisting of two parts, the platform and the payload. For more than one robot, we can use a standardized platform, with different payloads.

Embedded system

Very-low-cost, high-performance microprocessor-based embedded systems enable wide applications. Most of these boards, complete 32-bit computers with memory and I/O, cost less than $50. Add-on boards provide GPS location finding, wifi and bluetooth connectivity, 3-axis gyros, a wide variety of sensors, and motor control, via PWM.

Advances driven by cellular phones and data systems have made available small powerful processors that rival a datacenter of a few years back. They are designed for communication, and include a variety of standard interfaces. The devices are multicore, meaning there is more than one cpu. They can include specialty cores such as floating point or digital signal processing, They have memory integrated with the cpu. They support analog as well as digital interfaces. The boards tend of be deck-of-cards size or smaller, and typically cost under $50. Some examples include the Arduinos, Maple, Raspberry Pi, and BeagleBone board.

A Microcontroller is a single chip cpu (or cpu's). memory, and I/O solution. Many different variations form a single cpu architecture (such as ARM), exist, giving the designer the flexibility to choose hardware to meet his or her requirements.

Raspberry Pi

The Raspberry Pi is a small, inexpensive, single board computer based on the ARM architecture. It is targeted to the academic market. The latest model uses the ARM v8-A 32/64 bit architecture, in the the Broadcom BCM2837 system-on-a-chip. This has has a 1.2 GHz quad core arm processor, a video GPU, and 1 gigabyte of RAM. It uses an external SD card for storage. It includes a video camera interface, and an image processing pipeline.

The Raspberry Pi runs the GNU/linux and FreeBSD operating systems. Due to the open source nature of the software, Raspberry Pi applications and drivers can be downloaded from various sites. It requires a single power supply, and dissipates 1.5 watts. It has multiple USB ports, and an Ethernet controller. It does not have a real-time clock, but one can easily be added. It outputs video in HDMI resolution, and supports audio input/output. I/O includes 17 general purpose I/O lines.

Although the RaspberryPi is not designed to be Rad hard, it showed a surprisingly good radiation tolerance in tests. It continued to operate through a dose of 150 krad (Si), with only the loss of USB connectivity.

The Pi Compute Module supports a 10 DOF IMU, an RTC, Analog to digital converters, a real time clock, a dedicated camera port, and supports the communication interfaces I2C, SPI, GPIO, Ethernet and USB.

Embedded gpu

A GPU is optimized for video data processing. It is very fast, but not as versatile as an CPU. It operates on its own data formats. It is optimized to be blazingly fast at what it does. Following the same path, multi-core GPU's can be built. In fact, these are now the basis for most of the World's supercomputers.

GPU's found application in arcade machines, games consoles, pc's, tablets, phones, car dashboards, tv's and entertainment systems. Most of the World's top Supercomputers are based on massive numbers of GPU's. This lead to the interesting concept of Cloud-based super-computing. With a cloud-based array of GPU's, the mobile robot will have available to it a supercomputer as a service. We can include a GPU on the robot itself in lieu of a standard cpu, but we will look at the trades in doing that in the context of the NIST architectural model, discussed later.

A GPU operates on graphics data. This differs in format from integers and floating point numbers. Graphics data can be integer or floating point. Generally, it is organized in 1 dimensional arrays (vectors) or multi-dimensional arrays. Since we will see later that we can under use our GPU to do general purpose processing, there is nothing special about the data format. Keep in mind, the GPU does not implement logic functions.

To use the GPU in this way, we basically have to reformulated our computational problem in terms of the graphics operations the GPU provides. The OpenCL language, widely used in GPU programming, is general purpose.

Besides the usual add, subtract, multiply, and divide, there are some unique operations for graphics data. This include min, max, average, among others. We could accomplish these with a quick couple of lines of code, but it is much faster, once we develop the opcode to do it. Also, in graphics processing, it is common to have multiple units working on multiple data with the same operation at the same time.

A GPU is a specialized computer architecture to manipulate image data at high rates. The GPU devices are highly parallel, and specifically designed to handle image data, and operations on that data. They do this much fastest than a programmed general purpose CPU. Most desktop machines have the GPU function on a video card or integrated with their CPU. Originally, GPU's were circuit card based. Now, they're chips, and increasingly, multicore chips. GPU operations are very memory intensive. The GPU design is customized to SIMD type operations.

The instruction set of the GPU is specific to graphics operations on block data. The requirements were driven by the demands of 2-D and 3-D video games on pc's, phones, tablets, and dedicated gaming units. As GPU units became faster and more capable, they began to consume more power (and thus generate more heat) than the associated CPU's. The GPU operations are typically memory intensive, so fast access to memory is critical.

A GPU is generally a dataflow architecture, as opposed to a control-flow, Von Neumann machine. The instructions executed depend on the inputs, to the extent that the order of execution is non-deterministic. On general purpose machines implementing graphics processing code, the behavior would be deterministic.

Although designed to process video data, some GPU's have been used as adjunct data processors and accelerators in other areas involving vectors and matrices, such as the inverse discrete cosine transform. Types of higher-level processing implemented by GPU's include texture mapping, polygon rendering, object rotation, and coordination system transformation. They also support object shading operations, data oversampling, and interpolation. GPU's find a major application area in video decoding. Building on this, GPU's enable advanced features in digital cameras such as facial recognition, or eye tracking. GPU's can be used to accelerate database operations such as gather and scatter, vertex operations. A vertex is where lines (or vectors) meet. GPU's are enabling the optical lane departure feature on cars, and will help to enable self-driving cars.

You can do general purpose computing on a GPU, although it may not be the ideal platform. It requires you to recast your computation in a way the GPU understands, which is to say, in terms of graphics. So, we might have to represent the data as a 2D or 3D object, that we can apply the GPU's operations on. GPU's are special purpose devices that have instruction sets that are not general purpose, and are intended specifically for graphics data processing, and problems that lend themselves to stream or vector processing. GPU's are stream processors, in that they operate in parallel on multiple data. Given the right problem, that is mapable into the GPU's architecture, a huge performance gain of orders of magnitude can be achieved, over regular CPU's.

The bottleneck to getting more than one processor to work on a given problem domain at one time is the communications. There is an upper bound in a bus-oriented, shared memory SMP systems, arising from the communication limit of the bus interconnect (a classic Shannon channel limit). Clusters of computers also suffer from an inter-processor communication limit, from the LAN-like interconnect. We can use a message passing approach, or shared memory for inter-processor communication. And keep in mind, each node of the architecture can be more than a single processor – we can have a mesh of meshes in a hierarchical fashion.

Another technique is to put multiple cpu/gpu units on a single chip, and use that as a node in a compute network. This is called Multicore technology. Multicore computer architecture uses two or more (up to 100's) of cpu's, configured into a multiprocessor on a single chip. Each cpu can fetch and execute its own instructions, and has a method to communicate with the other cpu's. If an embedded chip has a cpu, memory, and I/O on a single chip, a multicore architecture has an entire network of parallel processors on a single chip. In the same sense that a computer used to fill a room, then was reduced to a box, then to a chip, we now see a further reduction of multiple cpu's. It's just Moore's law. Every 18 months or so, the technology can give us a 2x factor of improvement.

Extensive code libraries exist for GPU's, and different problem domains, from physics modeling, to video gaming and virtual reality. API's include OpenGL and Directx. OpenGL, the Open (source) graphics libraries operate across languages and platforms. It was introduced in 1992. It is an industry standard, and claims scalability from hand-held to supercomputer. It consists of a series of library functions, callable from most computer languages. DirectX, similarly, has a set of runtime libraries. It is a Microsoft product. There are other libraries of graphics functions available as well.

Embedded GPU's give us supercomputer-class computational ability, at the cost of power, usually, tens of watts. Their value on a mobile platform is in path planning. Due to the interest in self-driving cars, most of what we need is now off-the-shelf.

Intel is currently in its 10th generation of GPU's. The first-gen unit, the Intel 740 dates to 1998, and was supported by OpenGL. By the fifth generation, in 2010, each execution engine had a 128 bit wide floating point unit, that executed four 32-bit operations per clock. By the eighth generation, each EU had dual SIMD-4 FPU's, with clock rates below a gigahertz.

Cuda (Compute Unified Device Architecture) is the dominant proprietary GPU product from Nvidia. To go along with the hardware, nVidia provided massively parallel CDA-c, OpenCL, and DirectCompute software tools. These support not only parallelization, but also debugging of parallel code. GPU-targeted code can be developed by the same process and with the same look-and-feel tools as CPU code. Nvidia's Nexus development environment supports Microsoft Visual Studio, and C++. MATLAB provides a Parallel Computing Toolbox. Nvidia pioneered the use of GPU accelerators in 2007. They come with a set of optimized libraries, and parallization tools.

Smart Sensors

Smart sensors include embedded processing. The IEEE Standard 1451 covers functions, communication protocols, and formats for smart sensors. Networked and wireless sensors are also covered. Moving the processing closer to the sensor offloads this task from the main computer, freeing up resources for other tasks. Sensor fusion is also applicable. This is the merging of inputs from different sensor types to achieve a better knowledge of a situation or event.

A group of sensors working together can be organized into a network. These can be an array of similar or identical sensors, or a group of sensors using different technologies to gather a more complete perspective of the sensed item of interest. The sensor network can be wired or wireless. The detection devices monitor the local conditions and perform a small local area surveillance, collect data, and translate the acquired raw data to usable information. The network can be rigidly preplanned, or ad-hoc and self-organizing. This latter approach involves swarms of sensors, not all of which need to be the same.

Sensor-nets are groups of autonomous (smart) sensors, distributed over a certain space. They are connected in a node-network architecture. The system can be wired, but is usually wireless, for convenience. Sensor nets have been used, for example, to monitor forest fires, and water quality. These little sensor systems have to be inexpensive, and have low power consumption. Loss of individual nodes does not greatly impact the system. A mobile platform cant be a node on a sensor-net.

Power Concerns, the Cost of Computation, and Communications

Generally, the computer hardware can be designed to minimize the amount of power it consumes. The next issue is to control the amount of power the software takes.

Embedded GPU's have the ability of making mobile robot systems much more capable. The trade-off is, they will require more power. If the robot relies on a cloud service for image recognition, for example, the cost of communication must be taken into account, and even whether communication is possible. The robot might be exploring a mine, for example. The power problem involves the power cost of mobility and computation. As was seen with the early Mars Rovers, it took more power to compute the next move, than to actually accomplish it. In addition, a mobile platform needs to recharge it's batteries now and then, with the options being solar, and returning to a charging station. As technology progresses, we will get better batteries, and lower power GPU's.

Power is a constrained resource onboard the robots, and must be carefully managed. We generally have rechargeable batteries, and solar arrays for a power source. The computer has to monitor and control the state-of-charge of the batteries, sometimes dropping everything else it is doing to charge the batteries.

We also have to consider the power usage of the computer, while executing programs. Most embedded cpu's have some power saving modes, that come in handy for your cellphone, for example. These modes have names like "sleep" and "standby." The manufacturers' data sheet will define these modes, and their power consumption, compared to normal operation. In addition, some computers can selectively shut down some memory or I/O resources to reduce power as well.

To control power usage, we first need to add instrumentation to measure it. The embedded processor needs to be able to monitor its own power consumption. On the test bench, we can establish the energy required to run an algorithm. From this data, we make decisions according to the current situation and state as to the correct approach to apply. What we have measured and computed is the energy cost of computation. This can be done by the same computer that is using the battery energy. We can also keep track of the power expended from the battery pack, and monitor the battery state-of-charge.

Let's look at a simple example of onboard data processing on a small imaging mission. Here we are taking consecutive images at a resolution of 5 megapixels. This is 40 megabits, at 8 bits per pixel. In Cubesats, you have a limited downlink bandwidth due to power issues, and you only have communications over land. Cubesat generally do not have the resources to utilize the Tracking and Data Relay Satellites at a higher orbit. This implies we need to know when we are over land. There are lots of ways to do this, but we could run a simple orbit model onboard with stored maps. The spacecraft takes images continuously, stores them onboard, and downlinks them when a receiver is available.

We could also consider doing some image processing onboard. The Raspberry Pi, Model B2, for example have an Image Processing pipeline separate from the main cpu. It is supported by an open source image processing library. We can implement various levels of data compressing on the image, or do image differencing, or process to only include "areas of interest." All of this is feasible, but involves a lot of computation, which, in turn, uses a lot of power. So, we might consider only doing the computations, on stored data, when the Cubesat is in sunlight. We can predict this, and it is relatively easy to sense.

We might run into a conflict between processing the images, and downlinking them, if the Cubesat is in sunlight, and over land. A housekeeping task for an onboard computer is to keep track of the state-of-charge of the battery's by measuring current in and current out.

Mobile Robot Computing Software

This section discusses the mobile robot software. Open source software is preferred. We present an operating system choice, applications software from the NASA environment, and clustering software. Most of what we need is already available for download, leaving the integration process as the major step.

Open Source versus Proprietary

This is a topic we need to discuss before we get very far into software. It is not a technical topic, but concerns your right to use (and/or own, modify) software. It's those software licenses you click to agree with, and never read. That's what the intellectual property lawyers are betting on.

Software and software tools are available in proprietary and open source versions. Open source software is free and widely available, and may be incorporated into your system. It is available under license, which generally says that you can use it, but derivative products must be made available under the same license. This presents a problem if it is mixed with purchased, licensed commercial software, or a level of exclusivity is required. Major government agencies such as the Department of Defense and NASA have policies related to the use of Open Source software.

Adapting a commercial or open source operating system to a particular problem domain can be tricky. Usually, the commercial operating systems need to be used "as-is" and the source code is not available. The software can usually be configured between well-defined limits, but there will be no visibility of the internal workings. For the open source situation, there will be a multitude of source code modules and libraries that can be configured and customized, but the process is complex. The user can also write new modules in this case.

Large corporations or government agencies sometimes have problems incorporating open source products into their projects. Open Source did not fit the model of how they have done business traditionally. They are issues and lingering doubts. Many Federal agencies have developed their own Open Source policies. The Open Source Initiative (www.opensource.org) maintains the definition of Open Source, and certifies licenses such as the NOSA.

The GNU General Public License (GPL) is the most widely used free software license. It guarantees end users the freedoms to use, study, share, copy, and modify the software. Software that ensures that these rights are retained is called free software. The license was originally written by Richard Stallman of the Free Software Foundation (FSF) for the GNU project in 1989. The GPL is a *copyleft* license, which means that derived works can only be distributed under the same license terms. This is in distinction to permissive free software licenses, of which the BSD licenses are the standard examples. Copyleft is in counterpoint to traditional copyright. Proprietary software "poisons" free software, and cannot be included or integrated with it, without abandoned the GPL. The GPL covers the GNU/linux operating systems and most of the GNU/linux-based applications.

A Vendor's software tools and operating system or application code is usually proprietary intellectual property. It is unusual to get the source code to examine, at least without binding legal documents and additional funds. Along with this, you do get the vendor support. An alternative is open source code, which is in the public domain. There are a series of licenses covering open source code usage, including the Creative Commons License, the gnu public license, copyleft, and others. Open Source describes a collaborative environment for development and testing. Use of open source code carries with it an implied responsibility to "pay back" to the community. Open Source is not necessarily free.

The Open source philosophy is sometimes at odds with the rigidized procedures evolved to ensure software performance and reliability. Offsetting this is the increased visibility into the internals of the software packages, and control over the entire software package. Besides application code, operating systems such as GNU/linux and bsd can be open source. The programming language Python is open source. The popular web server Apache is also open source.

Keep in mind, executing software consumes energy and requires time. This can be observed and measured. A key issue is the development of a program style, and the development of a programming mindset; specifically. how will I debug this? This is the Design for Testability approach. It is similar to the Design for Test approach in hardware, where test points are provided at the design level.

Choice of Language

The choice of implementation language is not critical. It is better to go with the skillset of the implementer's, than dictate a particular language. C, C++, Java is acceptable. Cobol is not.

Linux

Linux is a family of free and open source operating systems, developed for the x86 architecture, but now widely available across platforms. Particularly, it supports the ARM architecture, and the embedded Raspberry Pi platform. Linux is not a real-time operating system in its standard form, but can be modified to be so. RTLinux is a hard real-time microkernal. There are variations of linux with different features, one of the more popular variants being Ubuntu. There are also enterprise level versions, and linux is found in many of the world's data centers and supercomputers. Linux is a variation of the Unix operating system, developed by Bell Labs.

Robot Operating System

The Robot Operating system is a collection of Open Source software and tools developed starting in 2007. It has been expanded to address teams of multiple robots, and real-time operations. ROS 2.0 is more of a middleware system, with extensive software libraries. Most interestingly, it includes the rosbridge3 package, which links the robot to an open source ROS environment in the Cloud.

Robot Operating System (ROS) is Open Source middleware that addresses robot applications. It is not a true operating system. It comes with extensive libraries in C++, Python, and LISP. Ubuntu linux is the preferred host OS. Other variants of linux, and Windows are partially supported. It can also run with Android. It has been integrated in a MATLAB toolbox. It provides services for computer clusters and cloud services (ROSbridge). This later software allows you to set up a cloud server, and link the robot via radio (such as wifi).

Packaged applications include perception, object identification, recognition, gesture recognition, and motion tracking. It supports stereo vision, and mobile robotics, as well as planning. It is supported on many hardware platforms, including Raspberry Pi. In addition, the canned Google Object Recognition Engine can be used.

RosJava is a java implementation of ROS, allowing for Android applications to be supported.

NASA's Core Flight Software

The Core Flight Executive from the Flight Software Branch at NASA/GSFC, is an open source operating system framework. The executive is a set of mission independent reusable software services and an operating environment. Within this architecture, various mission-specific applications can be hosted. The cFE focuses on the commonality of flight software. The Core Flight System (CFS) supplies libraries and applications. Much flight software legacy went into the concept of the cFE. It has gotten traction within the Goddard community, and is in use on many flight projects, simulators, and test beds. (FlatSats) at multiple NASA centers. But the key thing to note is, the software is fairly generic, and can be used in other areas, and for other missions, not just for space. It's first non-NASA application was for a drone.

The cFE presents a layered architecture, starting with the bootstrap process, and including a real time operating system. At this level, a board support package is needed for the particular hardware in use. Many of these have been developed. At the OS abstraction level, a Platform support package is included. The cFE core comes next, with cFE libraries and specific mission libraries. Ap's habituate the 5th, or upper layer. The cFE strives to provide a platform and project independent run time environment.

The boot process involves software to get things going after power-on, and is contained in non-volatile memory. cFE has several boot loaders available. The real time operating systems can be any of a number of different open source or proprietary products, VxWorks, RTEMS, or ROS for example. This layer provides interrupt handling, a scheduler, a file system, and inter-process communication.

The Platform Support Package is an abstraction layer that allows the cFE to run a particular RTOS on a particular hardware platform. There is a PSP for desktop pc's for the cFE. The cFE Core includes a set of re-usable, mission independent services. It presents a standardized application Program Interface (API) to the programmer.

A software bus architecture is provided for messaging between applications.

The Event services at the core level provides an interface to send asynchronous messages, telemetry. The cFE also provides time services.

Aps include a Health and Safety Ap with a watchdog. A housekeeping AP for messages with the ground, data storage and file manager aps, a memory checker, a stored command processor, a scheduler, a checksummer, and a memory manager. Aps can be developed and added to the library with ease.

The cFE has been released into the World-Wide Open Source community, and has found many applications outside of NASA.

The cFS is the core flight software, a series of aps for generally useful tasks onboard the spacecraft. The cFS is a platform and project independent reusable software framework and set of reusable applications. This framework is used as the basis for the flight software for satellite data systems and instruments, but can be used on other embedded systems in general. More information on the cFS can be found at http://cfs.gsfc.nasa.gov/OSAL

The OS Abstraction Layer (OSAL) project is a small software library that isolates the embedded software from the real time operating system. The OSAL provides an Application Program Interface (API) to an abstract real time operating system. This provides a way to develop one set of embedded application code that is independent of the operating system being used. It is a form of middleware.

cFS aps

CFS aps are core Flight System (CFS) applications that are plug-in's to the Core Flight Executive (cFE) component. Some of these are discussed below.

CCSDS File Delivery (CF)

The CF application is used for transmitting and receiving files. To transfer files using CFDP, the CF application must communicate with a CFDP compliant peer. CF sends and receives file information and file-data in Protocol Data Units (PDUs) that are compliant with the CFDP standard protocol defined in the CCSDS 727.0-B-4 Blue Book. The PDUs are transferred to and from the CF application via CCSDS packets on the cFE's software bus middleware.

Limit check (LC)

The LC application monitors telemetry data points in a cFS system and compares the values against predefined threshold limits. When a threshold condition is encountered, an event message is issued and a Relative Time Sequence (RTS) command script may be initiated to respond/react to the threshold violation.

Checksum (CS)

The CS application is used for for ensuring the integrity of onboard memory. CS calculates Cyclic Redundancy Checks (CRCs) on the different memory regions and compares the CRC values with a baseline value calculated at system start up. CS has the ability to ensure the integrity of cFE applications, cFE tables, the cFE core, the onboard operating system (OS), onboard EEPROM, as well as, any memory regions ("Memory") specified by the users.

Stored Command (SC)

The SC application allows a system to be autonomously commanded 24 hours a day using sequences of commands that are loaded to SC. Each command has a time tag associated with it, permitting the command to be released for distribution at predetermined times. SC supports both Absolute Time tagged command Sequences (ATSs) as well as multiple Relative Time tagged command Sequences (RTSs).

Scheduler (SCH)

The SCH application provides a method of generating software bus messages at predetermined timing intervals. This allows the system to operate in a Time Division Multiplexed (TDM) fashion with deterministic behavior. The TDM major frame is defined by the Major Time Synchronization Signal used by the cFE TIME Services (typically 1 Hz). The Minor Frame timing (number of slots executed within each Major Frame) is also configurable.

File Manager (FM)

The FM application provides onboard file system management services by processing ground commands for copying, moving, and renaming files, decompressing files, creating directories, deleting files and directories, providing file and directory informational telemetry messages, and providing open file and directory listings. The FM requires use of the cFS application library.

Software Agents

A software agent is a computer program that acts on behalf of a user. These are sometimes called "bots." Intelligent agents exhibit some form of artificial intelligence, enhanced autonomy and learning behavior. Autonomous agents are capable of modifying their approach to solving problems, or completing their task. Agents are distinguished from a regular software program, in that an agent is not explicitly invoked but runs continuously in the background It may stay in a wait state until needed. It does not require human intervention, but does have access to the computer's resources. Agents are defined by their behavior.

Self-Monitoring Agent

A Self-monitoring Agent is an approach that is running on the system it is testing. From formal testing results, and with certain key engineering tools, we can come up with likely failure modes, and possible remediation's. Besides self-test, we can have cross-checking of systems. Not everything can be tested by the software, without some additional hardware. First we will discuss the engineering analysis that will help us define the possible hardware and software failure cases, and then we will discuss possible actions and remediation's None of this is new, but the suggestion is to collect together best practices in the software testing area, develop a library of routines, and get operational experience.

The software has many diverse pieces, and is not just one module, but can be dispersed. Some of the modules run continuously and some are triggered on demand, due to a specific event. It is desirable to have as much fault/failure coverage as possible, while minimizing the impact on the host's memory and timing.

You're way ahead when you have some idea what is likely to fail, derived from testing, industry reports, case studies, and past history. Fault coverage has to be as complete as possible, and we should ensure we have the known failure modes covered. Of course, some failures were missed in testing, resulting in their presence becoming known in the operational environment. This information can be globally accessed from the Cloud.

It is also critically important to know exactly what software has been loaded into the robot computer. Version control should be in place from the beginning of the project.

There is also now a general policy of "test what you deploy, deploy what you test." You might have included diagnostic code for integration testing, and pull it out before deployment. Wrong. Now the code you are going to use is untested. The tested version includes the instrumentation code. Even though it will never be used, it takes up some memory space, so cache footprints, memory boundary's, and pipeline contents are different.

We also need to carefully consider the failure recovery. Sometimes, we will need the system to reboot itself. That's disruptive, but necessary in some cases. We want to take every possible path before going down that one.

CPU failures are fairly rare, but the computer may be operating in a hostile environment. There are known failure modes in this environment, that have to be covered. Failures will be transient or hard. Sometimes, hard failures result in a state that is not recoverable. Transient failures, on the other hand, are the hardest to find. We can observe the results, and try to work backward to the root cause. That is where good up-front analysis and data from system test is invaluable. Some architectures, such as the ARM Cortex-R7 have built-in hardware failure detection. That's a good approach, but it still leaves many potential failures uncovered.

We can tap industry best practices code for system testing. We can also use testing code developed for system POST (power-on-self-test) as an example. POST is accomplished after a reset, but before the system begins to run operational code. It does allowed for checking internal functionality. POST should certainly be included in our repertoire. POST doesn't have specific run time requirements (except the annoyance threshold). A large block of memory can be tested in sections, to avoid adversely affecting system timing.

The results of the monitoring software goes back to the cloud server. If there are multiple robotic units, the cloud server compares results in the case of another unit failure, to be able to predict a similar failure or fault in the other units.

Embedded AI

Embedded artificial intelligence and embedded deep learning are being deployed. Both required supercomputer-level computing, and we used to get that from the Cloud, but that's not a problem in the embedded world today. One application that has been deployed is Apple's Face ID, a biometric authentication system that runs on a phone. It is hosted on a custom System-on-a-Chip architecture, and is capable of 600 giga-operations per second. The chip is named the A11 Bionic engine. The system uses the front facing camera to map 30,000 points in the infrared spectrum. Apple has a library of apps for this, including the iOS imaging SDK. ARM developed the hardware, and is able to use it on its generic designs. In the ARM context, it is called DynamIQ, and runs on the ARM Cortex A chips.

Google is implementing a platform to host deep learning algorithms on ARM. At the moment, the hard work is done in the Cloud, but this has issues with privacy. When the relevant search is done on your device, it is easier to control the security aspects. A company called Reality AI is developing machine learning software libraries for embedded use.

Voice controlled assistants such as Amazon's Echo and Google Home now use cloud services to parse the verbal input. Current generation GPU's have the ability to do this, in situ. What the local units will not have, but will have access to, are the large databases, now hosted in the Cloud.

Cluster Software

There are many options for clustering software, that allow individual units to come together to work on one problem. One of these is Beowulf, free and open source, developed at NASA's Goddard Space Flight Center. It was intended to link commodity desktop pc's into a powerhouse computer. It runs under the linux operating system, and a version for the Raspberry Pi is available. It includes the Message Passing Interface, and a Parallel Virtual Machine. There is a server node, and some number of client nodes. In a swarm architecture, the mothership or cloud host could be the server node. The links, for mobile robot platforms, would be RF (or, perhaps, laser). The performance of the cluster depends on the capabilities of the individual nodes, as well as the communications infrastructure. A cluster computer acts like one big virtual supercompuer computer, with the individual members "hidden" to the user.

The Cloud

Cloud Computing refers to a virtualized compute and data storage center, accessible via high-bandwidth network connections. Its location is irrelevant to the applications. Cloud computers provide utility computing services – units of computation on demand or on reserve. Administration of the data center and the virtual resources are centralized, and become part of the cost of services. This approach provides economy of scale to computer utilization. It allows company's to have large computing resources without the overhead of maintaining them. The computing or data services are delivered as services over a network.

Cloud Computing is economical because it allows sharing of the hardware resources without sharing the data. There's nothing magic going on. People who know what they're doing build, maintain, and manage the data center and its resources. If you're good at building widgets, not computing, you can buy computing as a service. This works because of the growth of high speed networks, mostly optical, driven by demand of the Internet.

Computing as a utility is the same concept as public utilities for water, electricity, gas, and, for that matter, the road network. These are resources that represent large capital investment, and provide services to multiple user's, who pay for their potion of use. Amazon is widely regarded as being a major driver of the concept of Cloud Computing. They needed large amounts of hardware and data to manage their business. But, most of the time they had excess capacity for the average case, because of the need to address the maximum case. Amazon deployed the Cloud Model in their own datacenters, and rented out excess capacity. Amazon Web Services is a utility. At Acme Widgets, where they are very good at what they do, their compute and data requirements are both platform and location independent. Amazon or a number of other facilities can rent them secure storage and as much compute time as they need when they need it. As with most commodities, the pricing model sets price by demand. At the end of the month, when every one does their accounting reports, computing is more expensive. Defer that by a week, and get better rates.

The Cloud model is scalable and elastic. It is easy to incorporate more hardware resources, and to power them down when they are not needed. They is enough spare hardware up and running to not only take care of peak demand, but to provide spares in case of failures. Virtual machines can be moved between compute platforms. A technique called load leveling monitors and optimizes the use of the hardware. This is the same process the electrical utilities use to determine that they have to bring additional generators online to meet peak air conditioning demand.

The National Institute of Standards and Technology issued a definition of Cloud Computing. This was authored by Peter Mell and Timothy Grance, and is NIST Special Publication 800-145 (September 2011). National Institute of Standards and Technology, U.S. Department of Commerce. It is a short document, available for download. It says,

The five essential characteristics they define are:

"On-demand self-service. A consumer can unilaterally provision computing capabilities, such as server time and network storage, as needed automatically without requiring human interaction with each service provider.

Broad network access. Capabilities are available over the network and accessed through standard mechanisms that promote use by heterogeneous thin or thick client platforms (e.g., mobile phones, tablets, laptops, and workstations).

Resource pooling. The provider's computing resources are pooled to serve multiple consumers using a multi-tenant model, with different physical and virtual resources dynamically assigned and reassigned according to consumer demand.

Rapid elasticity. Capabilities can be elastically provisioned and released, in some cases automatically, to scale rapidly outward and inward commensurate with demand. To the consumer, the capabilities available for provisioning often appear to be unlimited and can be appropriated in any quantity at any time.

Measured service. Cloud systems automatically control and optimize resource use by leveraging a metering capability at some level of abstraction appropriate to the type of service (e.g., storage, processing, bandwidth, and active user accounts). Resource usage can be monitored, controlled, and reported, providing transparency for both the provider and consumer of the utilized service."

Service Models

Software as a Service (SaaS). The capability provided to the consumer is to use the provider's applications running on a cloud infrastructure. The applications are accessible from various client devices through either a thin client interface, such as a web browser (e.g., web-based email), or a program interface. The consumer does not manage or control the underlying cloud infrastructure including network, servers, operating systems, storage, or even individual application capabilities, with the possible exception of limited user-specific application configuration settings.

Platform as a Service (PaaS). The capability provided to the consumer is to deploy onto the cloud infrastructure consumer-created or acquired applications created using programming languages, libraries, services, and tools supported by the provider.3 The consumer does not manage or control the underlying cloud infrastructure including network, servers, operating systems, or storage, but has control over the deployed applications and possibly configuration settings for the application-hosting environment.

Infrastructure as a Service (IaaS). The capability provided to the consumer is to provision processing, storage, networks, and other fundamental computing resources where the consumer is able to deploy and run arbitrary software, which can include operating systems and applications. The consumer does not manage or control the underlying cloud infrastructure but has control over operating systems, storage, and deployed applications; and possibly limited control of select networking components (e.g., host firewalls).

Deployment Models

Private cloud. The cloud infrastructure is provisioned for exclusive use by a single organization comprising multiple consumers (e.g., business units). It may be owned, managed, and operated by the organization, a third party, or some combination of them, and it may exist on or off premises. This applies to mobile cloud services as well.

Community cloud. The cloud infrastructure is provisioned for exclusive use by a specific community of consumers from organizations that have shared concerns (e.g., mission, security requirements, policy, and compliance considerations). It may be owned, managed, and operated by one or more of the organizations in the community, a third party, or some combination of them, and it may exist on or off premises.

Public cloud. The cloud infrastructure is provisioned for open use by the general public. It may be owned, managed, and operated by a business, academic, or government organization, or some combination of them. It exists on the premises of the cloud provider.

Hybrid cloud. The cloud infrastructure is a composition of two or more distinct cloud infrastructures (private, community, or public) that remain unique entities, but are bound together by standardized or proprietary technology that enables data and application portability (e.g., cloud bursting for load balancing between clouds)."

You can access your "data in the cloud" from a client on a smartphone or tablet, or small robot. No big desktop computer is required. At the same time, you can use these small appliances to log into your cloud-based virtual computer cluster, and control the running of programs with a simple application at your end. If the Cloud host is a GPU-based supercomputer, you have access to awesome compute power.

The technical aspects of Cloud Computing are simple and well understood. The implications and the business models are still evolving.

Security in the Cloud

There is naturally a concern about sending your data and proprietary programs off somewhere nebulous. Cloud-based systems require new and innovative security measures. Cloud security is a barrier to adoption for many users.

The issues of physical security for the cloud facility is well understood from previous architectures of large data centers and data repositories. The issue of secure data access can also be addressed, but this is a more serious concern. As with any system, absolute security cannot be achieved. Layered security and threat assessment provide levels of security for Cloud centers that are comparable to commercial and military standards for protection of physical and data resources.

Cloud robotics needs enhanced security, to avoid the scenario where the remote robot units can be hijacked by malicious users, via their communication links. This can be addressed by continuous authentication over the comm link, which, of course, adds to the communication bandwidth problem.

In Cloud systems in general, and cloud robotics specifically, we can apply the principles of trust establishment, and trust measurement. In the trivial case, a correct password establishes trustworthiness.

Cloud Robotics

Cloud Robotics applies cloud techniques to robotic systems. We are not discussing factory operations here, but rather mobile robots, a harder problem. In cloud robotics, the robot platform benefits from the computer resources and storage space of "the cloud." The mobile robot platform communicates with its cloud over RF links. Multiple robot units, up to and including swarms, can use the cloud as a method of sharing information Humans can interact with the cloud to give directions, and observe the data. The mobile robots become "smarter." The cloud machine can implement and support a large data center and knowledge base, detailed dynamic task planners (using modeling), and deep learning from sensed data.

The architecture for the application of Cloud robotics in a production facility is obvious. There is a large server connected to various robotic workstations via high speed cable. That's almost a no-brainer.

The more difficult problem is with a mobile swarm. Here, the communication links are RF or optical. The architecture can be one mother unit in the swarm, with all other units being subservient, or all can be peers. All platforms would be built to a common hardware and software architecture. The mother unit, or super-node can provide cloud services to the swarm. There is a trade-off in computation, communication, and power consumption as to whether the cloud provides services to the other members, or whether the entire ensemble organizes into the cluster of convenience. In that case, we have what we might cal a "distributed cloud."

The idea is that the mothership has more storage and computational resources than any other member of the group, and can provide those services in a cloud environment, but the various members of the group can also be organized into one big compute engine, essentially a virtual cloud.

In one usage scenario, we have a mother unit with a swarm of exploration units, that operate with top-level supervision (World Model level). Each platform, built as a bus unit with mobility, electrical power, and compute resources would be common among units. Each would carry different sensing instrumentation. The exploration units would implement the lowest levels of the hierarchy, the software that interfaces with the sensors and actuators. The Cloud hosting machine implements the top level, the world model, and the interaction between units. Levels in-between may be hosted in either environment.

Each member of the swarm has a unique identifier. This is used in several ways to differentiate each unit. Each can have a metal QR tag affixed. This allows for over 2,900 binary bits. Other units can read and identify the unit optically. In addition, each unit can broadcast its unique number via a modulated LED. This will have the format of standard asynchronous serial communication – a start bit, n data bits, a parity bit, and a stop bit. N data bits allow for 2^n units. This would be in response to a "who are you?" query.

Cloud robots are operating now. Google self-driving cars are one example of mobility as a service, moving the intelligence out of the vehicle, and into the cloud. The Tesla Autopilot is another. The Society of Automotive Engineers defines 6 levels of autonomy of driving:

Level 0: Automated system issues warnings and may momentarily intervene but has no sustained vehicle control. (Most modern cars, circa 2017, include this feature.)

Level 1 ("hands on"): Driver and automated system shares control over the vehicle. An example would be Adaptive Cruise Control (ACC) where the driver controls steering and the automated system controls speed. Using Parking Assistance, steering is automated while speed is manual. The driver must be ready to retake full control at any time. Lane Keeping Assistance (LKA) Type II is a further example of level 1 self driving. (again, deployed in new vehicles by 2017).

Level 2 ("hands off"): The automated system takes full control of the vehicle (accelerating, braking, and steering). The driver must monitor the driving and be prepared to immediately intervene at any time if the automated system fails to respond properly. The shorthand "hands off" is not meant to be taken literally. In fact, contact between hand and wheel is often mandatory during SAE 2 driving, to confirm that the driver is ready to intervene.

Level 3 ("eyes off"): The driver can safely turn their attention away from the driving tasks, e.g. the driver can text or watch a movie. The vehicle will handle situations that call for an immediate response, like emergency braking. The driver must still be prepared to intervene within some limited time, specified by the manufacturer, when called upon by the vehicle to do so. In 2017 the Audi A8 Luxury Sedan was the first commercial car to claim to be able to do level 3 self driving. The car has a so-called Traffic Jam Pilot. When activated by the human driver, the car takes full control of all aspects of driving in slow-moving traffic at up to 60 kilometers per hour. The function works only on highways with a physical barrier separating oncoming traffic.

Level 4 ("mind off"): As level 3, but no driver attention is ever required for safety, i.e. the driver may safely go to sleep or leave the driver's seat. Self driving is supported only in limited areas (geo-referenced) or under special circumstances, like traffic jams. Outside of these areas or circumstances, the vehicle must be able to safely abort the trip, i.e. park the car, if the driver does not retake control.

Level 5 ("steering wheel optional"): No human intervention is required. An example would be a robotic taxi or truck.

(courtesy, Wikipedia)

Compute cluster of convenience

Within the system, we can implement co-operative computing, with a goal of reducing message volume to suite the capabilities of the system, while still returning information of value. This approach will be implemented with the Beowulf clustering software, and networking resources across the swarm. The workload is distributed across the swarm, to the extent that the task is parallelizable. The cluster can develop ad hoc, when its capabilities are needed. Pulling together the compute resources of multiple platforms to tackle a big job depends more on the communication capabilities available. Message relay might be used, but is probably too slow to consider for compute tasks. It also depends on the nature of the problem, and how much data has to be interchanged, how often. If individual units can be assigned a block of work (and associated data), that they work on independently, the system can handle that.

The Beowulf software was developed to provide a low cost open source solution to linking commodity pc's into a supercomputer. The approach has been applied to clusters of small architectures. As part of a student summer program, we demonstrated a 5 node cluster, using Raspberry Pi's. Several 64-node clusters have been constructed. These are the size of desktop pc's. Cluster computing has two parameters: Compute rate, in instructions/second, and data rate, in words/second. Generally, if these are in balance, we get the optimal results. A good design point is a balance in MIPS/MHz or GIPS/GHz (measured in instructions per data word). This depends, however, on the nature of the problem implemented on the cluster. An alternative to the cluster is cloud services, concentrated in the Mothership.

The Beowulf cluster is ideal for sorting and classifying data; an example application is the Probabilistic Neural Network. This algorithm has been used to search for patterns in remotely sensed data. It is computationally intensive, but scales well across compute clusters. It was developed by the Adaptive Scientific Data Processing (ASDP) group at NASA/GSFC. The program is available in Java source code.

Onboard databases

Each member of the Swarm is self-documenting. It carries a copy of its Electronic Data Sheet (EDS) description, which can be updated. This defines the system architecture and capabilities, and has both fixed (as-built) and variable entries. The main computer in the Mothership has a copy of these, and can get updates by query. The Mothership also has parameters on each unit's state, such as electrical power remaining, temperature, etc. One value of the database is, if the mothership needs a particular unit with a high resolution imager, it knows what unit that is, and whether it has been deployed or not. If it has been deployed, it can query the unit on its position and health status. Implementing the EDS in a true database has advantages, since the position of the data item in the database also carries information. It also allows the use of off-the-shelf database tools. The individual units have a "light-weight" version of the database, while the mothership has a more sophisticated one. All the schema's are the same.

There are two parts of the tables, representing static and dynamic data. Static Data represents the hardware and software configuration of the swarm unit. These values are not expected to change during the unit's operation. The Dynamic Data table represents the sensors each particular unit has. These values can change, and with a timestamp the last values will be kept as a part of the EDS during the mission.

The Mothership is responsible for aggregating all of the remote units housekeeping and science data, and transmitting it back to base. This is also facilitated by the structure imposed by the database. An Open Source version of an SQL database is preferred. The EDS documents will be in XML.

Science Data Processing

Generally, sensed data is sent unprocessed, because of the lack of computing resources on the mobile platform.. In some cases, there is not enough bandwidth to send the volume of data acquired, and it is stored onboard the robot, which returns to base. We can look at NASA's model for science data processing.

Data Processing Levels

NASA Earth Data products are processed at various levels from Level 0 to Level 4. Level 0 products are raw data at full instrument resolution. At higher levels, the data are converted into more useful parameters and formats. Instruments may produce data at any of these levels. This is the domain of NASA's Earth Observing System Data and Information System (EOSDIS), a large data processing facility dedicated to Earth Science at GSFC. These are their definitions:

Data Level 0

Reconstructed, unprocessed instrument and payload data at full resolution, with any and all communications artifacts (erg., synchronization frames, communications headers, duplicate data) removed. In most cases, the EOS Data and Operations System (EDOS) provides these data to the data centers as production data sets for processing by the Science Data Processing Segment (SDPS) or by a SIPS to produce higher-level products.

Data Level 1A

This is reconstructed, unprocessed instrument data at full resolution, time-referenced, and annotated with ancillary information, including radiometric and geometric calibration coefficients and geo-referencing parameters (e.g., platform ephemeris) computed and appended but not applied to Level 0 data

Data Level 1B

This is Level 1A data that have been processed to sensor units (not all instruments have Level 1B source data)

Data level 2

is geophysical variables at the same resolution and location as Level 1 source data.

Data Level 3

This has variables mapped on uniform space-time grid scales, usually with some completeness and consistency.

Data Level 4

This is model output or results from analyses of lower-level data (e.g., variables derived from multiple measurements).

Scientists have always advocated for sending only raw data, doing no onboard processing. Now, it is easy to implement the first several levels of instrument data onboard, and send higher level products. This has the advantage of requiring less bandwidth, and increasing the science data flow. Processing to Level 2 is certainly feasible.

Communication among members

Communications among members of the swarm or group is probably rf. For short distances, infrared can be used, if line-of-sight can be maintained. Short range radio such as Bluetooth or wifi can be used in restricted volumes.

The main communications link is seen to be radio, unit-unit, or via a ad-hoc wifi net set up by a the mothership. For longer distances, with intervening obstacles, a relay system might be needed. The communications protocols can be based on those of wireless networks, and wireless roaming. However, a delay tolerant protocol will be needed if significant amounts of information must be guaranteed to be interchanged. The ad hoc network for the computer cluster of convenience must be fast, and non-blocking. We may need, depending on the models, pro-active routing, where automatic periodic exchange of messages to every possible network destination are maintained, as are the routing tables. Ad-hoc routing uses a dynamic route (like the internet, and ethernet systems), and send messages only when it is necessary.

Gossip protocols are applicable to cloud robotics. They do not use route discovery, but can result in a high-latency in the network.

An Architectural Model

This section will discuss a hierarchical architectural model for a multi-robot systems, using a cloud architecture.

Real Time Control System (RCS)

NASA/NBS Standard Reference Model for Telerobot Control Systems Architecture (NASREM), was an early model for the implementation of advanced control architectures. It was used for the control architecture for NASA's Flight Telerobotic Servicer, which was never implemented. The compute architectures of the time, in the rad-hard configuration, were not up to the requirements. A telerobot control system could be implemented in the first 3 (of 7) levels of the NASREM model. Further levels could be added later in a phased evolution of the system. For early systems, the human operator provided the functionality of the upper control levels. Using a Cloud-based robotics system has its problems, mostly due to latency. Sometimes, real-time is required.

4D/RCS evolved from NASREM over decades, starting in the 1970's It is currently at RCS Level 4. RCS is a Reference Model Architecture for real-time control. It provides a framework for implementation in terms of a hierarchical control model derived from best theory and best practices. RCS was heavily influenced by the understanding of the biological cerebellum. NIST maintains a library of RCS software listings, scripts and tools, in ADA, Java, and C++.

An abstraction, the "perfect join"t accepts analog or digital torque commands, and produces the required torque via a dc motor. It also provides state feedback in the form of force, torque, angle or position, (depending on whether the joint configuration is Cartesian or revolute), and possibly rate. The perfect joint includes a pulse width modulator (pwm), a motor, and possibly a gearbox. Internal feedback and compensation is provided to compensate for gearbox or other irregularities such as hysteresis or stiction, For example, the torque pulses common to harmonic drives can be compensated for within the perfect joint. The perfect joint is part of the lowest NASREM level. The processing provided theoretically achieves a "perfect" torque, where the outputted torque matches the commanded torque.

NASREM had a 6-level model. Each layer of the model has defined interfaces, and it is designed for growth and expansion. It has a global database. Each level has three processes, the sensor processing, the world model, and the execution. The lowest level of the model, the primitive, has the bare metal sensors and actuators. Up form level from that is the primitive, or elementary move level, then task, service bay, and mission level. The world model is maintained by each level, and information moves between level. At the lowest level, is raw sensor data, At the highest level are the task plans and priorities. All of this is based on a common database format.

Each level of the model has distinct time horizons, and timing. The top level would strive to maintain about a planning horizon of about an hour.

In the case of the Mars Rovers, the earliest used pre-planned motions, which sometimes did not survive contact with reality. It is impossible to operate the units tele-robotically, due to the time delay, so sensing, re-planning, and commanding took hours. Later, the planning took place on the vehicle itself, following a master plan, but re-evaluating the plan based on video and other sensor data. In the NASREM model, a human might be located at the top of a hierarchy, making it a tele-operated system.

4D/RCS provides a conceptual framework for intelligent systems, a reference model for system components, implementation tools, and defines the human interface. It has been used for military unmanned vehicles architectures. 4D/RCS is a deliberative agent architecture. Agents can be autonomous, or work collaboratively with other agents.

4D/RCS integrates the NIST RCS with the University of Munich's VaMoRs-4 dynamic machine vision approach. It implements increasing levels of platform autonomy. It has transcended the control of single vehicles, to coordinating groups of vehicles. The operation of these vehicles have been demonstrated in DARPA's Grand Challenge, and Urban Grand Challenge. At the top level, up to 160 distinct platforms can be coordinated.

The hierarchy of 4D/RCS is similar to that of NASREM, but consists of 8 levels. As this is currently a military project, the levels have military organization names. The lowest level is the servo level, interfacing with sensors and actuators. The primitive level handles multiple actuator and sensor groups, and the dynamic interactions between them. A the subsystems level, co-ordination between subsystem elements is defined. At the "vehicle" level, what I called the platform level, all the subsystems are coordinated to achieve a behavior. At the "section" level, multiple vehicles are coordinated. At the platoon level, multiple sections of 10 or more vehicles of possibly different types are coordinated to desired tactics. At the "company" level, multiple platoons of 40 or more vehicles are coordinated for defined, platoon-level tactics. At the battalion level, units of 160 or more vehicles are coordinated for platoon-level tactics.

Even level 6 is capable of handling a swarm of robots. It is interesting to note that with a given sensor platform, in the satellite context, a "payload," different platforms, land, water, underwater air, could be substituted, keeping the payload intact.

Standards

There are many Standards applicable to Robotic and Cloud systems. These range from general computer standards to specific platform, communications, and security standards. Why should we be interested in standards? Standards represent an established approach, based on best practices. Standards are not created to stifle creativity or direct an implementation approach, but rather to give the benefit of previous experience. Adherence to standards implies that different parts will work together. Standards are often developed by a single company, and then adopted by the relevant industry. Other Standards are imposed by large customer organizations such as the Department of Defense, or the automobile industry. Many standards organizations exist to develop, review, and maintain standards.

Standards exist in many areas, including hardware, software, interfaces, protocols, testing, system safety, security, and certification, and Standards can be open or closed (proprietary). It is generally a good idea to see what standards are available and consider using them.

The issue of the security of cloud-based applications and data needs to be addressed.

Wrap-up

As it becomes easier to provide Cloud Services to a mobile collection of robots, that collection will become more versatile. We assume the units will be operating independently, or cooperatively, with global goals. In the simplest case, the Cloud provides a place for individual units to store data. The master unit will host cloud services, and serve a a classical data repository. It will be able either to provide compute services to the collection, or assemble them into a cluster of convenience to address big compute problems. We have to assess the communication bandwidth, and whether the main unit will act as a communication relay. We have to decide whether any unit can talk to any other directly, or whether all communications go through the master. We have to consider power sources and operating duration for all units. We also need to address communications security. Almost all of these requirements, when properly stated, will have off-the-shelf solutions. Mobile Cloud Robotics is not the future, it is now.

Bibliography

Albus, James A. *Brains, Behavior and Robotics*, McGraw-Hill Inc., 1st Edition, December 1, 1981, ISBN-10: 0070009759.

Albus, J. S "System Description and Design Architecture for Multiple Autonomous Undersea Vehicles," NISTTN 1251, National Institute of Standards and Technology, Gaithersburg, MD, September 1988.

Albus, J. S. "4D/RCS A Reference Model Architecture for Intelligent Unmanned Ground Vehicles," Proceedings of the SPIE 16th Annual International Symposium on Aerospace/Defense Sensing, Simulation and Controls, Orlando, FL, April 1–5, 2002

Albus, James et al. 4D/RCS: A Reference Model Architecture For Unmanned Vehicle Systems, Version 2.2, NIST, August 2002.

Antonopoulos, Nick and Gillam, Lee (Ed) *Cloud Computing: Principles, Systems and Applications*, Springer; 1st ed, August 2010, ISBN-1849962405.

Barlas, Gerassimos *Multicore and GPU Programming: An Integrated Approach,* Morgan Kaufmann, 1st ed, 2014, ISBN-978-0124171374.

Bradshaw, Jeffrey M. *Software Agents*, 1997, AAAI Press, ISBN-0262522349.

Bonabeau, Eric; Dorigo, Marco; Theraulaz, Guy *Swarm Intelligence: From Natural to Artificial Systems*, 1999, ISBN-01951315-2.

Bräunl, Thomas *Embedded Robotics: Mobile Robot Design and Applications with Embedded Systems* Springer; 2nd ed., 2006, ISBN- 3540343180.

Cafaro, Massimo (Ed) and Aloisio Giovanni, (Ed) *Grids, Clouds and Virtualization*, Springer; 1st ed, Sept, 2010, ISBN- 0857290487.

Cai, Yiyu; See, Simon *GPU Computing and Applications*, Springer, 2015, ISBN-978-9811013607.

Castellanos ,Jose A.; Tardós, Juan D. *Mobile Robot Localization and Map Building: A Multisensor Fusion Approach,* Springer; 2000 ed , 2000, ISBN- 0792377893.

Challa, Obulapathi N., McNair, Janise "Distributed Data Storage on Cubesat Clusters," Advances in Computing 2013, (3) 3 pp.36-49. Avail: *https://icubesat.files.wordpress.com/.../icubesat-org_2013-b-1-2-distributeddata_chall...*

Chapman, Barbara, et al Parallel Computing: From Multicores and Gpu's to Petascale (Advances in Parallel Computing), 2010, ISBN-10-1607505290.

Cook, Gerald *Mobile Robots: Navigation, Control and Remote Sensing,* Wiley-IEEE Press; 1st ed, 2011, ISBN-0470630213.

Dudek, Gregory; Jenkin, Michael *Computational Principles of Mobile Robotics* Cambridge University Press; 2nd ed, 2010, ISBN-0521692121.

Eliot, Lance *New Advances in AI Autonomous Driverless Self-Driving Cars: Artificial Intelligence and Machine Learning*, 2017, ISBN-0692048359.

Eliot, Dr. Lance; Eliot, Michael *Autonomous Vehicle Driverless Self-Driving Cars and Artificial Intelligence: Practical Advances in AI and Machine Learning*, 2017, ISBN-0692051023.

Elkady, Ayssam "Robotics Middleware: A Comprehensive Literature Survey and Attribute-Based Bibliography" Journal of Robotics, 2012. doi:10.1155/2012/959013.

Engelbrecht, Andries P. *Fundamentals of Computational Swarm Intelligence*, 2005, ISBN 0470091916.

Everett, H. R. *Sensors for Mobile Robots*, 1995, CRC Press, ISBN 1568810482.

Fallon, Michael *Self-driving Cars: The New Way Forward*, 2018, ISBN-1541500555.

Fortino, Giancarlo (Ed); Trunfio, Paolo (Ed) *Internet of Things Based on Smart Objects: Technology, Middleware and Applications,* 2014, ISBN-3319004905.

Ge, Shuzhi Sam Autonomous *Mobile Robots: Sensing, Control, Decision Making and Applications,* CRC Press, 2006, ISBN-0849337488.

Gudi, S. L.; Krishna Chand; Ojha, S.; Johnston, B.; Clark, J.; Williams, M.; "Fog Robotics for Efficient, Fluent and Robust Human-Robot Interaction," 2018, IEEE 17th International Symposium on Network Computing and Applications (NCA), November 2018, ISBN 978-1-5386-7659-2.

Guizzo, Erico "Cloud Robotics: Connected to the Cloud, Robots Get Smarter,"

2011,https://spectrum.ieee.org/cloud-robotics

Hall, John "maddog"; Gropp, William *Beowulf Cluster Computing with Linux*, 2003, ISBN -0262692929.

Hassanien, Aboul Ella; Emary, Eid *Swarm Intelligence: Principles, Advances, and Applications,*2015, ISBN-1498741061.

Hennemann, Christina *Google vs. Apple. Comparing Different Strategies to Establishing Self-Driving Cars*, 2017, ISBN-3668460388.

Hinchey, Michael G. ; Rash, James L.; Truszkowski, Walter E.; Rouff, Christopher A., Sterritt, Roy *Autonomous and Autonomic Swarms,* avail: https://ntrs.nasa.gov/search.jsp?R=20050210015 2017-12-20T20:19:24+00:00Z.

IEEE, "A Survey of Research on Cloud Robotics and Automation," 2015, IEEE Transactions on Automation Science and Engineering, Vol 12, Issue 2, pp. 398-409.

Hu, Guoqing; Tay, Wee Pasng; Wen, Yonggang; "Cloud Robotics: Architecture, Challanges and Applications," IEEE Network, V. 26, Issue 3.

avail: http://ieeexplore.ieee.org/document/6201212/

Jaulin, Luc (ed); Le Bars, Fabrice (ed), *Robotic Sailing 2013: Proceedings of the 6th International Robotic Sailing Conference,* Springer; Softcover reprint of the original 1st ed. 2014 edition ISBN-10: 3319033794.

Kindratenko, Volodymyr V. et all, "GPU Clusters for High-Performance Computing,"

avail:
www.ncsa.illinois.edu/People/kindr/papers/ppac09_paper
.pdf

Kehoe, Ben;Patil, Sachin; ABBeel, Pieter; Goldberg, Ken " A Survey of Research on Cloud Robotics and Automation," IEEE T. Automation Science and Engineering, Vol. 12, No. 2, April 2015.

Kirianaki, Nikolay V. et al *Data Acquisition and Signal Processing for Smart Sensors,* 2002, Wiley, ISBN 0470843179.

Koubaa, Anis *Robot Operating System (ROS): The Complete Reference* (Volume 2), 2017, ISBN-331954926X.

Li, Zhongkui; Duan, Zhisheng *Cooperative Control of Multi-Agent Systems: A Consensus Region Approach,* 2014, ISBN-1466569948.

Lipsom, Hod; Kurman, Melba *Driverless: Intelligent Cars and the Road Ahead,* MIT Press, 2016, ASIN-B01K13FURS.

Martinez, David R.; Bond, Robert A. *High Performance Embedded Computing Handbook: A Systems Perspective,* 2008, ISBN-084937197X.

Mead, Carver *Analog VLSI and Neural Systems,*1989, ISBN-0201059924.

Newman, Wyatt, *A Systematic Approach to Learning Robot Programming with ROS,* 2017, ISBN-1498777821 .

Pfister, Cuno *Getting Started with the Internet of Things: Connecting Sensors and Microcontrollers to the Cloud,* O'Reilly Media; 1st edition, June 2, 2011, ISBN-1449393578.

Plekhanova, Valentina *Intelligent Agent Software Engineering,* 2002, ISBN-1591400465.

Shroff, Gautam *Enterprise Cloud Computing: Technology, Architecture, Applications,* Cambridge University Press; 1st edition, Nov, 2010, ISBN-0521137357.

Spaanenburg, Lambert, and Spaanenburg, Hendrik *Cloud Connectivity and Embedded Sensory Systems* Springer; 1st ed, Dec., 2010, ISBN-1441975446.

Stakem, Patrick H. *Earth Rovers: for Exploration and Environmental Monitoring,* 2014, PRRB Publishing, ASIN BOOMBKZCBE.

Stakem, Patrick H. *Architecture of Massively Parallel Microprocessor Systems,* 2011, PRRB Publishing, ISBN-9781520250069.

Stakem, Patrick H. *Multicore Computer Architectures,* 2014, PRRB Publishing, ISBN-9781520241371.

Stakem, Patrick H. "The Brilliant Bulldozer: Parallel Processing Techniques for Onboard Computation in Unmanned Vehicles", 15th AUVS Symposium, San Diego, Ca. June 6-8, 1988.

Stakem, Patrick H.; Chandrasenan, Vishnu; Sinha, Surbhit; Mitra, Yash *A Cubesat Swarm Approach for the Exploration of the Asteroid Belt and Planetary Surfaces*, to be presented at the NASA-Goddard Planetary Cubesat Conference, Fall-2018.

Storti, Duane; Yurtoglu, Mete, *CUDA for Engineers: An Introduction to High-Performance Parallel Computing*, Addison Wesley Professional, 1st ed, 2015, 978-0134177410.

Tan, Ying *GPU-based Parallel Implementation of Swarm Intelligence Algorithms,* 2016, 1st ed Morgan-Kaufmann, ISBN-978-0128093627.

Truszkowski, Walt; Clark, P. E.; Curtis, S.; Rilee, M. Marr, G. "ANTS: Exploring the Solar System with an Autonomous Nanotechnology Swarm," J. Lunar and Planetary Science XXXIII (2002)

Velte, Toby, Elsenpeter, Robert *Cloud Computing, A Practical Approach*, McGraw-Hill Osborne Media; 1st edition, Sept, 2009, ISBN- 0071626948.

Tan, Ying *GPU-based Parallel Implementation of Swarm Intelligence Algorithms*, 2016, 1st ed, Morgan Kaufmann, ISBN-978-0128093627.

Wolf, Wayne, *High-Performance Embedded Computing: Architectures, Applications, and Methodologies*, Morgan Kaufmann, 2006, ISBN- 978-0123694850.

Resources

http://goldberg.berkeley.edu/cloud-robotics/

http://roboearth.org/cloud_robotics/

The Rise of Cloud Robotics, avail:

https://www.huffingtonpost.com/adi-gaskell/the-rise-of-cloud-robotic_b_9726370.html.

http://www.asme.org/engineering-topics/articles/robotics/6-ways-cloud-robotics-change-world.

Cloud Robotics: Architecture, Challenges and Applications, May 2012, IEEE Network 26(3):21-28.

http://www.myrobots.com/wiki/Cloud_Robotics.

http://www.idt.mdh.se/kurser/ct3340/ht11/MINICONFE
RENCE/FinalPapers/ircse11_submission_20 .pdf

http://searchcio.techtarget.com/opinion/Cloud-robotics-could-be-an-AI-game-changer.

www.ros.org

openrov.com

RCS: The Real-Time Control System Architecture, avail:

https://www.nist.gov/intelligent-systems-division/rcs-real-time-control-systems-architecture

4D/RCS: A Reference Model for Unmanned Vehicle Systems, Version 2.0, 2002, NIST
avail: http://ws680.nist.gov/publication/get_pdf.cfm?pub_id=821823

http://www.c2ro.com

RoboEarth: A World Wide Web for Robots, IEEE Spectrum, 2011, avail:

https://spectrum.ieee.org/automaton/robotics/artificial-intelligence/roboearth-a-world-wide-web-for-robots

Wikipedia, various.

NIST Bibliography

Mell, Peter; Grance, Timothy *NIST Definition of Cloud Computing*, 2011, SP-800-145.

V.D. Hunt, *Smart Robots: A Handbook of Intelligent Robotic Systems*, Chapman and Hall, 1985, ISBN-041200531X .

J. Vertut and P. Coiffet, *Teleoperation and Robotics Evolution and Development*, Prentice Hall, 1984, ISBN-9400789130.

C. Flatau, "Compact Servo Master-Slave Manipulation with Optimized Communication Links," Proc. of 17th RSTD Conference 1969, p. 154.

D.E. Whitney, "Resolved Motion Rate Control of Manipulators and Human Prostheses," IEEE Trans. Man-Machine Systems MMS- 10, 1969, p. 47.

R.P. Paul, "Manipulator Path Control," IEEE Int. Conf. on Cybernetics and Society, New York,

R.P. Paul, "Manipulator Cartesian Path Control," IEEE Trans. Systems, Man, Cybernetics SMC-9, 1979,

R.P. Paul, *Robot Manipulators: Mathematics, Programming, and Control*, MIT Press, 1981, ISBN-026216082X.

R. H. Taylor, "Planning and Execution of Straight-line Manipulator Trajectories," IBM J. Research and Development 23 1979, p. 424.

M. Hollerbach. "A Recursive Formulation of Lagrangian Manipulator Dynamic" IEEE Trans. Systems. Man. Cybernetics SMC-lO, 11, 1980, p. 730.

J.Y.S. Luh, M.W. Walker, and R.P.c. Paul, "On-line Computational Scheme for Mechanical Manipulators," J. Dynamic S)'stems. Measurement. Control, 102, 1980,

C.S.G. Lee, P.R. Chang, "Efficient Parallel Algorithm for Robot Inverse Dynamics Computation," IEEE Trans. on Systems. Man and Cybernetics, Vol. SMC-16, No.4, July/August 1986,

E.E. Binder, J.H. Herzog, "Distributed Computer Architecture and Fast Parallel Algorithm in Real-Time Robot Control," IEEE Trans. on Svstems. Man and Cybernetics, Vol. SMC-16, No. 4, July/August 1986,

M.H. Raibert and J.1. Craig, "Hybrid position/force control of manipulators," J. Dynamic Systems. Measurement. Control, June, 1981, p. 126.

H. Kazerooni, T.B. Sheridan, P.K. Houpt, "Robust Compliant Motion for Manipulators, Part I: The Fundamental Concepts of Compliant Motion," JEEE Journal of Robotics and Automation, Vol. RA-2, No.2, June 1986, p. 83.

H. Kazerooni, P.K. Houpt, T.B. Sheridan, "Robust Compliant Motion for Manipulators, Part II: Design Method," IEEE Journal of Robotics and Automation, Vol. RA-2, No.2, June 1986, p.93.

W. Hamel and M. Feldman, "The Advancement of Remote Technology: Past Perspectives and Future Plans," Proc.1984 National Topical Meeting on Robotics and Remote Handling in Hostile Environments, ANS, Gatlinburg, TN, April, 1984.

J. Albus, C. Mclean, A. Barbera, M. Fitzgerald, " An Architecture for Real-Time Sensory-Interactive Control of Robots in a Manufacturing Environment," 4th IFACIIFIP Symposium on Information Control Problems in Manufacturing Technology, Gaithersburg, Oct., 1982.

J T. Hong and M. Shneier, "Describing a Robot's Workspace Using a Sequence of Views from a Moving Camera," IEEE Trans. PAMI, vol PAMI-7, no. 6,1985, p. 721.

P. Brown, "The Interactive Process Planning System," 1986 Winter ASME Conf., Anaheim, Dec., 1986 (submitted).

W.A. Perkins, "A Model Based Vision System for Industrial Parts," IEEE Trans. on Computers, Vol. C-27, 1978, p. 126.

G.L. Gleason, G.J. Agin, "A Modular Vision System for Sensor-controlled Manipulation and Inspection," Proc. 9th Int. Symposium on Industrial Robots, 1979, p. 57.

J. E. Kent, M. Nashman, P. Mansbach, L. Palombo, M.A. Shneier, "Six Dimensional Vision System," SPIE, Vol. 336, Robot Vision, 1982, p. 142.

R.C. Bolles, R.A. Cain, "Recognizing and Locating Partially Visible Objects: The Local Feature-Focus Method," Int. Journal of Robotics Research, Vol. 1, 1982, p. 57.

T.F. Knoll and R.C. Jain, "Recognizing Partially Visible Objects Using Feature Indexed Hypotheses," Proc. IEEE Conf. on Robotics and Automation, San Francisco, 1986. p.925.

C. Crowley, "Navigation for an Intelligent Mobile Robot," IEEE Journal of Robotics and Automation, Vol. RA-l, No.1, 1985, p. 31.

R. Lumia, "Representing Solids for a Real-Time Robot Sensory System," Proc. Prolamat 1985, Paris, June 1985.

M.O. Shneier, E.W. Kent, P. Mansbach, "Representing Workspace and Model Knowledge for a Robot with Mobile Sensors," Proc. 7th Int. Conf. Pattern Recognition, 1984. p. 199.

M. A.. Shneier, R. Lumia, E.W. Kent, "Model Based Strategies for High Level Robot Vision," <u>CVGIP</u>, Vol. 33,1986, p. 293.

A. Barr, E. Feigenbaum, *The Handbook of Artificial Intelligence*, Kaufman, 1981, ASIN-B01DSRU4

C. McLean, "An Architecture for Intelligent Manufacturing Control." <u>1st ASME Computers in Engineering Conf.</u>, Boston, Aug., 1985.

Glossary of Terms

5C – connection, conversion, cyber, cognition, configuration.

Abandonware – software product, no longer supported

Accumulator – a register to hold numeric values during and after an operation.

ACM – Association for Computing Machinery; professional organization..

Aerostat – flight system deriving lift from buoyancy.

Aerobot – aerial robot

Agent – an autonomous entity (hardware/software) which is goal-seeking.

AI – artificial intelligence.

AML – Agent Modeling Language

ANTS – Autonomous Nano Technology Swarm

ALU – arithmetic logic unit.

Android – an operating system based on Linux, popular for smart phones and tablet computers.

ANSI – American National Standards Institute

API – application program interface; specification for software modules to communicate.

ARM – Acorn RISC machine; a 32-bit architecture with wide application in embedded systems.

ARPA – Advanced Research Projects Agency.

ASCII - American Standard Code for Information Interchange, a 7- bit code; developed for teleprinters.

Assembly language – low level programming language specific to a particular ISA.

Async – asynchronous; using different clocks.

Atmosat – platform operating at high altitude in the atmosphere, for extended periods.

Autonomous – self-governing.

Baud – symbol rate; may or may not be the same as bitrate.

BCD – binary coded decimal. 4-bit entity used to represent 10 different decimal digits; with 6 spare states.

Beowulf – clustering technology for linux-based computers.

Big-endian – data format with the most significant bit or byte at the lowest address, ortransmitted first.

Binary – using base 2 arithmetic for number representation.

BIOS – basic input output system; first software run after boot.

BIST – built-in self test.

Bit – smallest unit of digital information; two states.

Blackbox – functional device with inputs and outputs, but no detail on the internal workings.

Blade Server – a streamlined single-board server computer for rack mount.

Boolean – a data type with two values; an operation on these data t ypes; named after George Boole, mid-19th century inventor of Boolean algebra.

without external intervention.

Bot – short for robot; usually refers to a software agent.

BSD – Berkeley Software Distribution version of the Bell Labs Unix operating system.

Buffer – a temporary holding location for data.

Bug – an error in a program or device.

Bus – data channel, communication pathway for data transfer.

Byte – ordered collection of 8 bits; values from 0-255

C – programming language from Bell Labs, circa 1972.

Cache – faster and smaller intermediate memory between the processor and main memory.

Cache coherency – process to keep the contents of multiple caches consistent

CFS – NASA/GSFC embedded open source software.

Chip – integrated circuit component.

Clock – periodic timing signal to control and synchronize operations.

Cloud Server – a virtual private server that can be modified during runtime, or moved to a different host.

Complement – in binary logic, the opposite state.

Compilation – software process to translate source code to assembly or machine code (or error codes).

Co-processor – another processor to supplement the operations of the main processor. Used for floating point, video, etc. Usually relies on the main processor for instruction.

COS – (cluster of work) stations.

Core – early non-volatile memory technology based on ferromagnetic toroids.

Cots – commercial, off-the-shelf.

Cps – cyber-physical system.

CPU – central processing unit.

Cubesat – small satellite standard architecture.

CUDA - Compute Unified Device Architecture, from Nvidia.

Daemon – in multitasking, a program that runs in the background.

Dalvik – the virtual machine in the Android operating system.

DARPA - (U. S.) Defense Advanced Research Project Agency.

Dataflow – computer architecture where a changing value forces recalculation of dependent values.

Datagram – message on a packet switched network; the delivery, arrival time, and order of arrival are not guaranteed.

DATMO – detection and tracking of other moving objects.

DAT network - Data Augmentation and Transferring.

DDR – dual data rate (memory).

Deadlock – a situation in which two or more competing actions are each waiting for the other to finish, and thus neither ever does.

Denorm – in floating point representation, a non-zero number with a magnitude less than the smallest normal number.

Device driver – specific software to interface a peripheral to the operating system.

Digital – using discrete values for representation of states or numbers.

Dirty bit – used to signal that the contents of a cache have changed.

DMA - direct memory access (to/from memory, for I/O devices).

Dof – degrees of freedom

DOI – digital object identifier.

Doubleword – two words; if word = 8 bits, double word = 16 bits.

DPS – distributed problem solving.

Dram – dynamic random access memory.

Drone – unmanned aerial vehicle.

DSN – NASA's Deep Space Network

DSP – digital signal processing.

EDS – Electronic Data Sheets.

EIA – Electronics Industry Association.

Embedded system – a computer systems with limited human interfaces and performing specific   tasks. Usually part of a   larger system.

Ethernet – 1980's networking technology. IEEE 802.3.

Exception – interrupt due to internal events, such as overflow.

Fetch/execute cycle – basic operating cycle of a computer; fetch the instruction, execute the instruction.

Firmware – code contained in a non-volatile memory.

Fixed point – computer numeric format with a fixed number of   digits or bits, and a fixed radix point. Integers.

Flag – a binary indicator.

Flash memory – a type of non-volatile memory, similar to EEprom.

Floating point – computer numeric format for real numbers; has significant digits and an exponent.

FPGA – field programmable gate array.

FPU – floating point unit, an ALU for floating point numbers.

Giga - 10^9 or 2^{30}

GPIO – general purpose input output

Gnu – recursive acronym; gnu (is) not unix. Operating system that is free software.

GPL – gnu public license used for free software; referred to as the "copyleft."

GPU – graphics processing unit. ALU for graphics data.

GPU cluster – compute nodes and fast interconnect, a classic MPMS.

Handshake – co-ordination mechanism.

Hexadecimal – base 16 number representation.

HDMI – High definition multimedia interface

Homeostasis – a self-moniotoring, self-regulating system.

HPC – high performance computing.

HSA – Heterogeneous System Architecture.

HTTP – hypertext transfer protocol

Hypervisor – virtual machine manager. Can manage multiple operating systems.

IaaS – Infrastructure as a service.

IDE – Integrated development environment for software; also a popular interface for storage devices such as disk and cd/dvd/

IEEE – Institute of Electrical and Electronic Engineers. Professional organization and standards body.

IEEE-754 – standard for floating point representation and operations.

IMU – inertial measurement unit.

Infinity - the largest number that can be represented in the number system.

Integer – the natural numbers, zero, and the negatives of the natural numbers.

Interrupt – an asynchronous event to signal a need for attention (example: the phone rings).

Interrupt vector – entry in a table pointing to an interrupt service routine; indexed by interrupt number.

I^2C – serial interface, inter-integrated circuit

I/O – Input-output from the computer to external devices, or a user interface.

IoT – Internet of Things.

IP – intellectual property; also internet protocol.

ISA – instruction set architecture, the software description of the computer.

ISD – Intelligent Systems Division, NIST

ISO – International Standards Organization.

ISR – interrupt service routine, a subroutine that handles a particular interrupt event.

ISS – International Space Station.

Java – programming language that targets the Java Virtual Machine.

JPEG - Joint Photographic Experts Group

Kernel – main portion of the operating system. Interface between the applications and hardware.

Kilo – a prefix for 10^3 or 2^{10}

LAN – local area network.

Latency – time delay.

LFRL - Lifelong Federated Reinforcement learning

Lidar – radar, using light. Same thing, different frequency.

Linux – unix-like operating system developed by Linus Torvalds; open source.

LISP – programming language for list processing (1958).

List – a data structure.

Little-endian – data format with the least significant bit or byte at the highest address, or transmitted last.

Logic operation – generally, negate, AND, OR, XOR, and their inverses.

Logo – programming language for education and robotics, based on LISP (1967).

Lorax - Life on Ice: Robotic Antarctic eXplorer.

Loop-unrolling – optimization of a loop for speed at the cost of space.

LRU – least recently used; an algorithm for item replacement in a cache.

LSB – least significant bit or byte.

LUT – look up table.

Machine language – native code for a particular computer hardware.

Mainframe – a computer you can't lift.

Malware – malicious software; virus, worm, Trojan, spyware, adware, and such.

Mantissa – significant digits (as opposed to the exponent) of a floating point value.

Math operation – generally, add, subtract, multiply, divide.

Mega - 10^6 or 2^{20}

Memory leak – when a program uses memory resources but does not release them, leading to a lack of available memory.

M2C - Machine-to-cloud

M2M – machine-to-machine.

Memory scrubbing – detecting and correcting bit errors.

MEMS - microelectronic mechanical systems – producing mechanical systems such as gyros using microelectronics fabrication technology.

Mesh – a highly connected network.

MESI – modified, exclusive, shared, invalid state of a cache coherency protocol.

Metaprogramming – programs that produce or modify other programs.

Microcode – hardware level data structures to translate machine instructions into sequences of circuit level operations.

Microcontroller – microprocessor with included memory and/or I/O.

Microprocessor – a monolithic cpu on a chip.

MIMD – multiple instruction, multiple data

Mips – millions of instructions per second; sometimes used as a measure of throughput; also, a RISC CPU chip (Microprocessor without Interlocked Pipeline Stages).

MMU – memory management unit; translates virtual to physical addresses.

MPE – Media Processing Engine.

MPEG – motion picture experts group – standards for audio and video compression and transmission.

MPI – message passing interface.

MSB – most significant bit or byte.

Multiplex – combining signals on a communication channel by sampling.

Mutex – a data structure and methodology for mutual exclusion.

Multicore – multiple processing cores on one substrate or chip; need not be identical.

NAN – not-a-number; invalid bit pattern.

NAND – negated (or inverse) AND function.

NASA – National Aeronautics and Space Administration.

NASREM - NASA/NBS Standard Reference Model for Telerobot Control Systems Architecture

NDA – non-disclosure agreement; legal agreement protecting IP.

MPE – Media Processing Engine.

MPEG – motion picture experts group – standards for audio and video compression and transmission.

Myrobots - a social network for robots., and smarty objects.

Nibble – 4 bits, ½ byte.

NIST – National Institute of Standards and Technology (US), previously, National Bureau of Standards.

NMI – non-maskable interrupt; cannot be ignored by the software.

NOAA – National Oceanographic Atmospheric Administration.

NOR – negated (or inverse) OR function.

Noos - cloud robotics service.

Normalized number – in the proper format for floating point representation.

NRE – non-recurring engineering; one-time costs for a project.

NSF – National Science Foundation.

Numa – non-uniform memory access for multiprocessors; local and global memory access protocol.

NVM – non-volatile memory.

ONR - Office of Naval Research.

Off-the-shelf – commercially available; not custom.

Opcode – part of a machine language instruction that specifies the operation to be performed.

Open source – methodology for hardware or software development with free distribution and access.

Operating system – software that controls the allocation of resources in a computer.

OSI – Open systems interconnect model for networking, from ISO.

Overflow - the result of an arithmetic operation exceeds the capacity of the destination.

PaaS – platform as a service.

Packet – a small container; a block of data on a network.

Paging – memory management technique using fixed size memory blocks.

PAI – Parallel AI

Paradigm – a pattern or model

Paradigm shift – a change from one paradigm to another. Disruptive or evolutionary.

Parallel – multiple operations or communication proceeding simultaneously.

Parity – an error detecting mechanism involving an extra check bit in the word.

PARL - Peer-assisted Robotic learning

Pc – personal computer, politically correct, program counter.

Peta - 10^{15} or 2^{50}

Petaflops – 10^{15} floating point operations per second.

Pipeline – operations in serial, assembly-line fashion.

Posix – portable operating system interface, IEEE standard.

Prox-ops – proximity operations.

ROS - robot operating system.

RTC – real time clock.

PVM – parallel virtual machine

PWM – pulse width modulation; used for dc motor speed control.

Python – programming language.

QR – Quick Response Code, 2 dimensional barcode pattern, machine readable.

Quad word – four words. If word = 16 bits, quad word is 64 bits.

Queue – first in, first out data buffer structure; hardware of software.

RAID – random array of inexpensive disks; using commodity disk drives to build large storage arrays.

Radix point – separates integer and fractional parts of a real number.

RAM – random access memory; any item can be access in the same time as any other.

RAPYuta - open source cloud robotics framework.

RCS – real-time control system; robot control system.

Register – temporary storage location for a data item.

Regolith - layer of unconsolidated rocky material covering bedrock.

Reset – signal and process that returns the hardware to a known, defined state.

RISC – reduced instruction set computer.

ROBO Earth - European Project.

ROM – read only memory.

Router – networking component for packets.

Real-time – system that responds to events in a predictable, bounded time.

RoboBrain - NSF project.

ROCOS - cloud robotics platform.

ROS – robot operating system.

SaaS – software as a service.

SAE – Society of Automotive engineers.

SATA – serial ATA, a storage media interconnect.

Sandbox – an isolated and controlled environment to run untested or potentially malicious code.

Script – a program for an interpreter. Used to automate tasks.

SDR – software defined radio.

SDRAM – synchronous dynamic random access memory.

Segmentation – dividing a network or memory into sections.

Semiconductor – material with electrical characteristics between conductors and insulators; basis of current technology processor and memory devices.

Semaphore –signaling element among processes.

Serial – bit by bit.

Server – a computer running services on a network.

Seu – single event upset in electronics, due to radiation.

Shift – move one bit position to the left or right in a word.

Sign-magnitude – number representation with a specific sign bit.

Signed number – representation with a value and a numeric sign.

SIMD – single instruction, multiple data.

SIMM – single in-line memory module.

SLAM – simultaneous localization and mapping

SOC – system on chip

Software – set of instructions and data to tell a computer what to do.

SMP – symmetrical multiprocessing.

SPI – serial peripheral interface

Snoop – monitor packets in a network, or data in a cache

SRAM – static random access memory.

Stack – first in, last out data structure. Can be hardware of software.

Stack pointer – a reference pointer to the top of the stack.

State machine – model of sequential processes.

Superscalar – computer with instruction-level parallelism, by replication of resources.

Synchronous – using the same clock to coordinate operations.

System – a collection of interacting elements and relationships with a specific behavior.

System of Systems – a complex collection of systems with pooled resources.

Table – data structure. Can be multi-dimensional.

Tera - 10^{12} or 2^{40}

Test-and-set – coordination mechanism for multiple processes that allows reading to a location and writing it in a non- interruptible manner.

TCP/IP – transmission control protocol/internet protocol; layered set of protocols for networks.

Thin Client – a computer that is primarily designed to interface   with a larger machine via networking.

Thread – smallest independent set of instructions managed by a multiprocessing operating system.

Thumb – an instruction set and operating mode for the ARM processor.

TLB – translation lookaside buffer – a cache of addresses.

Transceiver – receiver and transmitter in one box.

Transputer – a microcomputer on a chip by Inmos Corp., circa 1980. Innovative communication mechanism using serial links.

TRAP – exception or fault handling mechanism in a computer; operating system component.

Truncate – discard.

TTL – transistor-transistor logic in digital integrated circuits. (circa 1963)

UAS – unmanned aerial system.

UaV – unmanned aerial vehicle, or remotely piloted aircraft, or drone.

Ubuntu – linux variant.

URDF – Unified Robot Description Format.

USB – universal serial bus.

Unsigned number – a number without a numeric sign.

UUV – unmanned underwater vehicle.

Vector – single dimensional array of values.

Virtual Appliance - a virtual machine image for a specific application.

Virtual memory – memory management technique using address translation.

Virtual private server – a virtual machine provided by an Internet hosting service.

Virtualization – creating a virtual resource from available physical resources.

Virus – malignant computer program.

VLIW – very long instruction word – mechanism for parallelism.

VxWorks – real time operating system from WindRiver Corp.

Wiki – the Hawaiian word for "quick." Refers to a collaborative content website.

Word – a collection of bits of any size; does not have to be a power of two.

Write-back – cache organization where the data is not written to main memory until the cache location is needed for re-use.

Write-through – all cache writes also go to memory.

WWW – World Wide Web.

XEN – Hypervisor, University of Cambridge, UK.

XOR – exclusive OR; either but not both.

Zero address – architecture using implicit addressing, like a stack.

If you enjoyed this book, you might also be interested in some of these.

16-bit Microprocessors, History and Architecture, 2013 PRRB Publishing, ISBN-1520210922.

4- and 8-bit Microprocessors, Architecture and History, 2013, PRRB Publishing, ISBN-152021572X,

Apollo's Computers, 2014, PRRB Publishing, ISBN-1520215800.

Architecture and Applications of the ARM Microprocessors, 2013, PRRB Publishing, ISBN-1520215843.

Earth Rovers: for Exploration and Environmental Monitoring, 2014, PRRB Publishing, ISBN-152021586X.

Embedded Computer Systems, Volume 1, Introduction and Architecture, 2013, PRRB Publishing, ISBN-1520215959.

The History of Spacecraft Computers from the V-2 to the Space Station, 2013, PRRB Publishing, ISBN-1520216181.

Floating Point Computation, 2013, PRRB Publishing, ISBN-152021619X.

Architecture of Massively Parallel Microprocessor Systems, 2011, PRRB Publishing, ISBN-1520250061.

Multicore Computer Architecture, 2014, PRRB Publishing, ISBN-1520241372.

Personal Robots, 2014, PRRB Publishing, ISBN-1520216254.

RISC Microprocessors, History and Overview, 2013, PRRB Publishing, ISBN-1520216289.

Robots and Telerobots in Space Applications, 2011, PRRB Publishing, ISBN-1520210361.

The Saturn Rocket and the Pegasus Missions, 1965, 2013, PRRB Publishing, ISBN-1520209916.

Visiting the NASA Centers, and Locations of Historic Rockets & Spacecraft, 2017, PRRB Publishing, ISBN-1549651205.

Microprocessors in Space, 2011, PRRB Publishing, ISBN-1520216343.

Computer *Virtualization and the Cloud*, 2013, PRRB Publishing, ISBN-152021636X.

What's the Worst That Could Happen? Bad Assumptions, Ignorance, Failures and Screw-ups in Engineering Projects, 2014, PRRB Publishing, ISBN-1520207166.

Computer Architecture & Programming of the Intel x86 Family, 2013, PRRB Publishing, ISBN-1520263724.

The Hardware and Software Architecture of the Transputer, 2011,PRRB Publishing, ISBN-152020681X.

Mainframes, Computing on Big Iron, 2015, PRRB Publishing, ISBN- 1520216459.

Spacecraft Control Centers, 2015, PRRB Publishing, ISBN-1520200617.

Embedded in Space, 2015, PRRB Publishing, ISBN-1520215916.

A Practitioner's Guide to RISC Microprocessor Architecture, Wiley-Interscience, 1996, ISBN-0471130184.

Cubesat Engineering, PRRB Publishing, 2017, ISBN-1520754019.

Cubesat Operations, PRRB Publishing, 2017, ISBN-152076717X.

Interplanetary Cubesats, PRRB Publishing, 2017, ISBN-1520766173 .

Cubesat Constellations, Clusters, and Swarms, Stakem, PRRB Publishing, 2017, ISBN-1520767544.

Graphics Processing Units, an overview, 2017, PRRB Publishing, ISBN-1520879695.

Intel Embedded and the Arduino-101, 2017, PRRB Publishing, ISBN-1520879296.

Orbital Debris, the problem and the mitigation, 2018, PRRB Publishing, ISBN-*1980466483.*

Manufacturing in Space, 2018, PRRB Publishing, ISBN-1977076041.

NASA's Ships and Planes, 2018, PRRB Publishing, ISBN-1977076823.

Space Tourism, 2018, PRRB Publishing, ISBN-1977073506.

STEM – Data Storage and Communications, 2018, PRRB Publishing, ISBN-1977073115.

In-Space Robotic Repair and Servicing, 2018, PRRB Publishing, ISBN-1980478236.

Introducing Weather in the pre-K to 12 Curricula, A Resource Guide for Educators, 2017, PRRB Publishing, ISBN-1980638241.

Introducing Astronomy in the pre-K to 12 Curricula, A Resource Guide for Educators, 2017, PRRB Publishing, ISBN-198104065X.

Also available in a Brazilian Portuguese edition, ISBN-1983106127.

Deep Space Gateways, the Moon and Beyond, 2017, PRRB Publishing, ISBN-1973465701.

Exploration of the Gas Giants, Space Missions to Jupiter, Saturn, Uranus, and Neptune, PRRB Publishing, 2018, ISBN-9781717814500.

Crewed Spacecraft, 2017, PRRB Publishing, ISBN-1549992406.

Rocketplanes to Space, 2017, PRRB Publishing, ISBN-1549992589.

Crewed Space Stations, 2017, PRRB Publishing, ISBN-1549992228.

Enviro-bots for STEM: Using Robotics in the pre-K to 12 Curricula, A Resource Guide for Educators, 2017, PRRB Publishing, ISBN-1549656619.

STEM-Sat, Using Cubesats in the pre-K to 12 Curricula, A Resource Guide for Educators, 2017, ISBN-1549656376.

Embedded GPU's, 2018, PRRB Publishing, ISBN-1980476497.

Mobile Cloud Robotics, 2018, PRRB Publishing, ISBN-1980488088.

Extreme Environment Embedded Systems, 2017, PRRB Publishing, ISBN-1520215967.

What's the Worst, Volume-2, 2018, ISBN-1981005579.

Spaceports, 2018, ISBN-1981022287.

Space Launch Vehicles, 2018, ISBN-1983071773.

Mars, 2018, ISBN-1983116902.

X-86, 40th Anniversary ed, 2018, ISBN-1983189405.

Lunar Orbital Platform-Gateway, 2018, PRRB Publishing, ISBN-1980498628.

Space Weather, 2018, ISBN-1723904023.

STEM-Engineering Process, 2017, ISBN-1983196517.

Space Telescopes, 2018, PRRB Publishing, ISBN-1728728568.

Exoplanets, 2018, PRRB Publishing, ISBN-9781731385055.

Planetary Defense, 2018, PRRB Publishing, ISBN-9781731001207.

Exploration of the Asteroid Belt, 2018, PRRB Publishing, ISBN-1731049846.

Terraforming, 2018, PRRB Publishing, ISBN-1790308100.

Martian Railroad, 2019, PRRB Publishing, ISBN-1794488243.

Exoplanets, 2019, PRRB Publishing, ISBN-1731385056.

Exploiting the Moon, 2019, PRRB Publishing, ISBN-1091057850.

RISC-V, an Open Source Solution for Space Flight Computers, 2019, PRRB Publishing, ISBN-1796434388.

Arm in Space, 2019, PRRB Publishing, ISBN-9781099789137.

Search for *Extraterrestrial Life*, 2019, PRRB Publishing, ISBN-978-1072072188.

Submarine Launched Ballistic Missiles, 2019, ISBN-978-1088954904.

Space Command, Military in Space, 2019, PRRB Publishing, ISBN-978-1693005398.

Robotic Exploration of the Icy moons of the Gas Giants, ISBN- 979-8621431006.

History & Future of Cubesats, ISBN-978-1986536356.

Robotic Exploration of the Icy Moons of the Ice Giants, by Swarms of Cubesats, ISBN-979-8621431006.

Swarm Robotics, ISBN-979-8534505948.

Introduction to Electric Power Systems, ISBN-979-8519208727.

Powerships, Powerbarges, Floating Wind Farms: electricity when and where you need it, 2021, PRRB Publishing, ISBN-979-8716199477.

Centros de Control: Operaciones en Satélites del Estándar CubeSat (Spanish Edition), 2021, ISBN-979-8510113068.

The Artemis Missions, Return to the Moon, and on to Mars, 2021, ISBN-979-8490532361.

James Webb Space Telescope. A New Era in Astronomy, 2021, ISBN-979-8773857969.